The Lonelin

P9-DTD-975

The Loneliness of Winter

BY

CANON SHEEHAN

THE MERCIER PRESS

CORK and DUBLIN

THE MERCIER PRESS, 4 Bridge Street, Cork
25 Lower Abbey Street, Dublin 1

This edition 1973

SBN 85342 330 X

PUBLISHERS NOTE

This is a reprint of part of Canon Sheehan's famous book *Under the Cedars and the Stars*. The remaining parts are published under the following titles:

The Magic of Spring

The Beauty of Summer

The Sadness of Autumn

CONTENTS

SECTION I.

SECTION II.

SECTION III.

SECTION I.

The Phosphorescence of decay

I notice these early evenings of winter a curious light in my garden; and across the river there is a faint twilight amongst the trees, so faint it is like the shadow of moonlight, or a terrestrial reflection of the Milky Way. I have read in some old book that it is the phosphorescence of decay. Everyone has seen the strange, pale light that accompanies the effluvia from decayed fish; and the beautiful phosphor-tinted waves which mariners gaze at, and poets rave about, in the incandescent tropical seas, are but the clear ocean waters heaving restlessly under a horrible burden of decomposition. This is realism with a vengeance! And, as I am a sworn foe to realism, and refuse to see aught but what I can idealize, I behold in the pale blue light that hangs above the dead forest-leaves, or the unctuous meteors from the leprous scum of the ocean, some idea of a soul, some promise of immortality. It is the poet's soul of Nature, framed from primeval fires and reverting, under paler conditions, to its original state; and taking with it, out of the decaying matter which once it vivified, the one element that ensures its own immortality.

Death

Death – the great mystery! You remember how Tolstoy forces it on Levin's vision in that dread *Anna Karènina*. It is so inevitable, so repulsive, that one yearns to find in it some hidden charm, some mercy, that will show even beneath its hideous features the eternal and unchangeable beauty, that is, the goodness of God. And now it is all around. Nature is dead. Bare trees, grassless fields, empty gardens, flowerless beds, gloomy skies, sunless days – ay, all is dead, dead! And, as you trample under foot these wet days in the early winter, great, soft masses of red leaves, rotting chestnuts, fallen acorns; and think of all the glories and generous promise of Spring, and all the luxuriant splendour of Autumn, the question involuntarily arises: *Ut quid perditio haec?* Wherefore this waste? Why all this prodigality of Nature for nothing? Where is the law of parsimony: *Entia non sunt multiplicanda sine necessitate!* Until you lift your eyes on high and see that this, too, is a law of Nature. Wherefore the eternal destruction and evolution of Nature – the construction and destruction of suns and planets? Wherefore the waste of light in the universe, if only an infinitesimal portion of our sun's light reaches his planets? And sound? And the never-ending vibrations of electricity? Is all this lost, and 'cast as rubbish to the void'? It cannot be. There is some explanation of the mystery.

The Garment of the Eternal

Ay, says the scientist, so there is. There is nothing lost, or mislaid in the universe. Matter is indestructible; so is force eternal! The perpetual interplay goes on, without haste, without rest – the never-ceasing weaving in the looms of Time of the garments of the Eternal! How do the verses go?

In the currents of life, in the tempests of motion,
In the fervour of act, in the fire, in the storm,
> Hither and thither,
> Over and under
> Wend I and wander.
> Birth and the grave,
> Limitless ocean,
> Where the restless wave
> Undulates ever,
> Under and over.
> Their seething strife,
> Heaving and weaving
> The changes of life.

10

At the whirling loom of Time unawed
I work the living mantle of God.

Ay, but that mantle is woven out of mists and shadows, out of clouds and rain, as well as out of suns and lightnings; and it is studded and hung around with humble bells and promegranates, as well as with the pearls of stars, or the fleeces of comets. And nothing is too mean to be rejected as contributory to the whole fabric and tissue of beauty. The widow's mite was acceptable in the temple; the grass grows greenest above the grave. There is a beauty in decay; there is a kind of glory in destruction, as of honour in creation. There is nothing lost. All is fair and beautiful in the end. Only, there must be an object – otherwise all is waste power, as of a gristless mill that grinds itself away. And that object clearly is the garment of the Eternal, the sacerdotal Vestments in which God is ever arrayed for the sacrifice that is never consummated.

No final loss, or failure

And, as in matter, so too in mind. In its eternal reproduction nothing is lost. It is impossible not to sympathize with what the world calls its failures. For every failure has in it the germ of a great success. Shakspere was unknown for one hundred and fifty years after his death. And many a titled booby whose horse he held outside that London theatre probably despised him as a potboy, and flung him a *pourboire* with contempt. Shelley was defunct for fifty years after his death; and Wordsworth for fifty years during his life. Dante lay dead for centuries; then he rose to immortality. All the celebrities of these centuries, contemporaries of these immortals, and overshadowing them with their borrowed splendours, have long ago passed out into the unknown. The failures have risen up to perfect and permanent success. So, too, even now. The great men of our age are unknown. They will be heard of in a century or two perhaps. A fashionable beauty at a watering-place will attract more attention than the young girl who has just won her gold medal in Greek or Science. Any skilful golfist is of more account than the Senior Wrangler. The loud-voiced, many-gestured demagogue occupies more space in public attention, and in the public press, than the silent student, who at midnight is building up great fabrics of thought for the future, or discovering some subtle solution for the political enigmata of the present. But in a different sense from that intended by the poet:

The One remains, the Many change and pass.

Thought is permanent; words evaporate. You cannot kill ideas, nor imprison them. Nay, you cannot oppose them, or contradict them, if they are built on the foundations of unalterable truth. And as the most forlorn and rejected things are taken up and woven in Nature's laboratory into all beautiful and glowing forms, so the silent thoughts of the unknown are woven into action by those who never heard the author's name, but who have been thrilled into doing under the spell of a voiceless inspiration.

Thought and Action

Hence, too, it would seem that the pen is greater than the voice. It lasts longer and reaches further. The *littérateur* is a greater power than the politician. He inspires the latter; and outlasts him. Rousseau precipitated the French Revolution; and survived it. He created Marat and Robespierre; they did not extinguish him. He will live when they are forgotten. So much the worse; but we are only noticing facts. Of the two great men who held the mind of England for the last half of the nineteenth century, the literary man will outlive the statesman. Newman will be an active and perennial force when Gladstone is but a name. The one left behind him thoughts; the other deeds. But thoughts are longer lived than deeds. So, too, moral teaching lasts longer than pure intellectualism, and is far more fertile of good. Superior intelligence does not win humanity. There never was such a silly comparison, even in the chaotic writings of unbelievers, as that which was instituted between Socrates and Christ – the one, a hard, cold, reasoning sophist; the other, the incarnation of tenderness and love. We soon get tired of that infinite wrapping and unwrapping of words in the dialogues of the former. We never weary of the tender pathos of the latter. Compare the Banquet where Socrates drank all the young men under the table, and went out to argue in his barren, disputative way in the streets; and the Last Supper, where Christ gave Himself to His Disciples, and, having sung a hymn, went forth to His Agony! Contrast the hard, mechanic, pettifogging question: Didst thou not say, Crito? with the 'soft wailings of infinite pity' – 'Filioli mei'; 'Jerusalem, Jerusalem, how often would I have gathered thy children'; 'Our friend, Lazarus, sleepeth'; 'Little children, love one another'; 'Simon Peter, lovest thou me?' 'Eloi, Eloi, lamma sabacthani?'

'Cataract Days'

Timanthes, unable to express the grief of Agamemnon at the death of Iphigenia, painted the father with head covered and face enveiled. And the sun, unable to bear the horror of the death of Nature, veils his face from us these short days of winter. Ay, indeed, they are dark days! Just a kind of mournful twilight between the night and the night. And what is worse, it is a weeping twilight. We have no cold until January and February; but drip! drip! drip! comes the rain all day long, flooding rivers, filling swamps, creating lakelets everywhere; and all night long it is the same soft swish of rain, rain, rain upon the roof, flooding the shoots beneath the eaves, dripping from the bare trees; and you can hear the channels running flooded to the river, and see the swollen river sweeping noiselessly to the sea. Oh, but is is dreary,

dreary, like the moated grange, and the 'rusted nail, that held the pear to the garden wall.' Yet these days, too, have their enjoyments. I confess I like a real, downright, wet day. Not one that is rainy by fits and starts, so that you must go out, and get muddy boots and dripping mackintosh; but a day when the conduits of the sky are turned on fully, and the great sheets come down steadily, steadily, or beat in fitful gusts against your windows, and wash them clean; and the most hopeful weather-prophet, scanning every quarter of the sky, cannot see the faintest break of cloud to warrant him in presaging that, sooner or later, it will clear. We have plenty of these 'cataract' days in Ireland; and they are simply delightful!

Their advantages

Delightful? Yes, to be sure. And first, you have the intense joy of unbroken solitude. You are alone – absolutely alone for a whole day! The knocker is muffled; the bell is silent. No foolish people who want to waste an hour on you, will venture forth to-day. Those who have real business to transact will defer it. Then your conscience is at rest. If you do stir up the fragrant woodfire, and watch the merry blazes dance up the deep chimney, and wheel over your armchair; and take up your latest purchase, crisp and clean from the publisher, or musty and stained from the second-hand 'catalogue,' there are no qualms about luxurious idleness; no thought of that country-school to be visited, or that horrid scandal to be unearthed, or that grimy lane to be patrolled. You cannot go out – that is all about it! There, listen! Swish go the cataracts; patter, patter go the bullets of rain on your windows! The whole landscape is blotted out in a mist of smoke; gray sheets of water are steered across the fields and trees by the jealous wind; little jets of brown liquid are thrown up from the puddles in the streets where the rain-drops strike them. The channels are choked with the eager running of the streamlets from the streets; the brown river sweeps majestically along. There is no use in trying. You *cannot* go out. Wheel your chair closer; watch for a moment, for the greater enjoyment, the desolation and death without. Then glance at the ruddy flame; and, finally, bury yourself deep, deep in your book. No fear of interruption; one two, three hours pass by in that glorious interchange of ideas. Life has nothing better to offer you. Enjoy it while you may!

Faded letters

How you would hate the miserable optimist, who, intruding on such sacred seclusion, would say with a knowing look: "Tis clearing away in the west! There is a break down there behind the trees! we'll have a fine afternoon!' Imagine, a sickly, pallid winter sun looking down on such a wet, bedraggled landscape; and, in unholy alliance with your conscience, ordering you away from that cheerful, neighbourly fire! And how you would bless the cheerful croaker, who, looking north, south, east, and west, would shake his head sadly, and say: 'No stirring abroad to-day! You wouldn't drive a dog from your door in such weather! We shall have forty-eight hours' continuous rain!' Forty-eight hours! Think of it! Think of it! How we will poke in long-forgotten drawers, and look up old accounts, and see how extravagant we were in our heyday, and examine old diaries, and re-read century-old letters. There, you took them up by chance, and now, entranced, you sit on the edge of a chair, or on an open trunk, and read, till your eyes grow dim with fatigue, or – tears. Ah! indeed, the letter, frayed and yellow, is almost falling to pieces in your hands. You hold it together with an effort. Letter by letter, the old familiar hand-writing begins to dawn on you, and you read. It is all 'dear,' or 'dearest,' and 'surely you must have known that I never intended to hurt,' and 'are you not over-sensitive, dear, and too prone to take offence,' and 'Come over informally this evening and let us forget.' You poise the letter in your fingers and try to remember. Yes! you wrote a dignified and very cutting letter in reply; and a great sea evermore rolled between you and the friend, whose face these many years has been upturned to the stars. Or it is a letter from a child at school, largely printed and ill-spelled, asking you for a little favour. You refused it, as a duty, of course, as if there were any duty to one another in this world but love. Or, it is from a poor friend, who has gone down in the struggle, and is in sore distress, and begs 'for auld lang syne' to help him. You could have spared that twenty or fifty dollars easily; but you were prudent. You argued: He is extravagant; 'tis his own fault. It will be a lesson to refuse him. Alas! you wouldn't have liked to see his face as he read your letter. He has long since sunk beneath the current; and his children are begging their bread. Well, fold it up, but don't burn it. It is a voice from the grave.

Kant and Fichte

I do not think there is any circumstance in the even life of Immanuel Kant, that is more painful to his admirers than his cold refusal of a few ducats to poor Fichte, to help the latter back to his native province. And I think there is hardly on record a more touching and dignified letter than this appeal of Fichte's wrung from him only by the direst distress. 'By a residence in my native province, I could most easily obtain, as a village pastor, the perfect literary quiet which I desire until my faculties are matured. My best course thus seems to be to return home; – but I am deprived of the means; I have only two ducats, and even these are not my own, for I have yet to pay for my lodgings. There appears then to be no rescue for me from this situation, unless I can find someone who, in reliance on my honour, will advance me the necessary sum for the expenses of my journey, until the time when I can calculate with certainty on being able to make repayment. I know no one to whom I could offer this security without fear of being laughed at to my face, except you... I am so convinced of a certain sacrifice of honour in thus placing it in pledge, that the very necessity of giving you this assurance seems to deprive me of a part of it myself; and the deep shame which thus fall upon me is the reason why I cannot make an application of this kind verbally, for I must have no witness of that shame. My honour seems to me really doubtful until that engagement is fulfilled, because it is always possible for the other party to suppose that I may never fulfil it.'

He never added, poor fellow, that in the background, behind the imagined vicarage, was the form of his betrothed, Johanna Rahn, who was only waiting for these reluctant ducats to become the faithful wife that she proved herself to be in all the after-years.

A refusal

Now it is quite certain that no one can read that letter without sharing the sense of shame that must have suffused the face of the writer, and tingled in his fingers as he wrote it. And no one can read of Kant's refusal – professor, scholar, and philosopher, as he was – without feeling equal shame. And yet how different are the sentiments. The one is the shame of great pity; the other, the shame of disappointment. We are sorry for Fichte, because he is reduced to so pitiable a condition even of honourable mendicancy; we are sorry for Kant, because of his 'lost opportunities.' But we could retain for ever the letter of the former, as a relic of honourable shame; we would gladly forget the refusal of the latter, as a stain on a great reputation.

L. S. D.

Ah me! those accounts – Dr. and Cr. and L.S.D.! What desperate plungers and wastrels we all were in our heyday! What a stoical contempt we had for money! That picture which we fancied, and which the dealer assured us was a real Van Dyck; that vast encyclopaedia; twelve guineas for that Tissot's Life of Christ, which we instantly gave away, because of its horrid French realism; that summer vacation – how that hotel bill did mount up! We shake our heads mournfully over ourselves – ourselves, mind, of the past, not ourselves of the present – there we are always devout idolaters! But those items – charity, 2s. 6d.; charity, 5s.; charity, 15s.; charity, 20s.; are these, too, regrettable? Happily, no! We cast our bread upon the running waters; and, after many days, it was returned.

Diaries

And these diaries! Dear me! How brief your life's history! Into how small a space have you concentrated the thoughts, ideas, desires, emotions, passions, that swayed you for so many years! That day, so full of hope, or shame, or sorrow, or ambition, or anxiety – how swiftly you have dismissed it in one line! You remember you thought it would never end. You thought that suspense intolerable, that affront unbearable, that injury irreparable. You took a despondent view of life, a despairful view of men. You said in your anger: *Omnis homo mendax!* How little it all looks now. What a speck in the vistas of years! How childish now seem your anger, your impatience, your fretfulness! How keenly you realize that the worst evils are those which never occur! You worked yourself into a fever of passion over possibilities. You saw ahead but rapids, and shallows, and rocks. Lo! your life has glided smoothly over all; and you smile at the perils that encompassed you. And that bitter disappointment – that misunderstanding which threatened such dire ruin to your prospects; lo! it has gone by harmlessly; and you are ashamed of your vindictiveness and hate and childish apprehensions. The great wave that came on threatening to engulf you, you have buoyantly surmounted; and you are out on the great high seas, whilst it has passed onward, and broken harmlessly on the shore.

'We look before and after, and pine for what is not' Foolish enough! Live in the present; and pull down a thick veil over the future, leaving it in God's hands. Live, live, in the present, sucking out of the hours of live all the honey they will yield.

Mors aurem vellens, 'Vivite,' ait, 'Venio.'

Their teachings

But there is a somewhat different lesson to be gathered from these same old, frayed, and yellow records of the past. I have purposely omitted the first line of the quotation, which runs thus:

Pone merum talosque; pereant qui crastina curant;
Mors aurem vellens, 'Vivite,' ait, 'Venio.'

I rather like that picture of grim Death, flicking the ear of his victim, and whispering: 'Make the most of it, old fellow, I'm coming for you soon.' But the 'pone merum talosque' sounds very like old Omar; and after all, this voluptuous life won't do. All men are agreed upon that, except that most miserable class of men of whom perhaps Des Esscintes in Huysman's novel is a type, and who closes his worthless, pleasure-seeking life by a fate that seems sufficient retribution: *Sur le chemin, dégrisé, seul, abominablement lassé.* Neither will it do to seek that milder Epicurean paradise in which, without labour or suffering, and merely by mental training and mind-abstraction, there is perfect and profound peace. I do not say that men should not practise mind discipline so perfectly that they can shake off easily the minor worries of life. This is very desirable. Nay, it should be a part of all education to teach that the will is paramount, that the minor faculties must obey it, and that a memory that loves to go back upon remorse, or an imagination that is prone to dwell on a perilous future, must be curbed by the superior power, and learn to abide in the present. But this is a long distance away from the religious peace connoted by the famous liner of St. Teresa:

Nada te turbe!	Let nothing trouble thee!
Nada te espante!	Let nothing frighten thee!
Todo se passa!	All things pass away.
Dios no se muda!	God alone is immutable!
La pacienza	Patience obtains every-
Todo lo alcanza	thing.
Quien a Dios tiene	He who possesses God
Nada te falta,	wants nothing:
Solo Dios basta!	God alone suffices.

Peace through Holiness

Philosophy has aimed at the former. Religion has secured the latter. That perfect peace – the Nirvana of the Asiatics has never been attained by mortal; cannot, indeed, be obtained until after the soul has migrated from being to being, and has become so attenuated that it has lost self-consciousness. To attempt this in ordinary life is to fail. It seems easy to say: Abstract your mind from all earthly things; let men be as shadows beneath you; live in the higher atmosphere of thought, and dwell alone with your own soul; let neither love, nor vanity, nor ambition, nor any earthly desire have place in your heart, and you will know what is meant by perfect peace. Alas! we have struck our roots too deeply into the earth to root them thus up remorselessly without pain; and the more we seek such peace, the further will it fly from us. What then? Is there something better? Something higher? No! there is nothing higher than perfect peace; but it must be peace through holiness. In other words, there is no use in abstracting ourselves from earth, if we cling to self. After all, it is self that torments us; and if we could wean ourselves from all things else, so long as self remains, there is no perfect peace.

Cardinal Newman

I was rather struck with this thought on reading Hutton's monograph on Cardinal Newman. It is not very interesting reading, because it is too philosophical, in the sense that it is too synthetic. We all like analysis of character – the drawing asunder and unravelling of the various threads that make up human life. But when an author begins to draw big conclusions on things in general from these threads, it is apt to weary. But it is wholesome to learn that the great Cardinal did, in early life, grasp the principle that 'Holiness is better than peace!' It seems a paradox, under one aspect, because we generally understand that peace is the concomitant or result of holiness. But the meaning clearly is that the soul that seeks peace without holiness will never find it; that life, an imperfect thing, is inseparable from trial; that difficulties are to be overcome, not to be avoided; that the soul that shrinks into itself behind the ramparts of philosophic thought will be discovered, and that cares will creep over the wall; and that, finally, it is only by self-abandonment and the annihilation of our own wills that we can foreshadow in life the peace of eternity. This is what the Lord meant when he said: '*My* peace I leave unto you; *My* peace I give unto you! Not as the world gives do I give unto you!'

The luxury of Unhappiness

Nevertheless, whilst all this is true, there are secondary helps in reflection which are not to be despised. And one of these comes from retrospection. Remorse for failures or mistakes is foolish. They are part and parcel of our imperfection. The past should not be allowed to cast a shadow of gloom on the present, nor to project itself across our future. But it has its lessons – the supreme one that anxiety is not only want of faith, but foolish in the extreme; and the other, a lesson of supreme gratitude to the merciful Providence who has ordered our lives so peacefully. The little souls that fume and fret under the little worries and vexations of life should often take up their diaries and read them. There they will see how trifling were the things that poisoned their daily happiness, how insignificant the grains of dust that made the discord of their lives. A little courage would have brushed that dust aside and restored the soul to harmony and happiness. But no! we preferred the luxury of knowing that we were unhappy, and grudged ourselves the little labour that would have restored concord and peace. Nay, most people nurse their miseries and help them to grow, as if they believed that the monotony of peace were undesirable, and that a life varied by vexations were preferable to a calm and equable existence, free from worry, and mapped without the red or black lines that connote disaster or suffering.

Hospitals

Then I would make such little souls walk the hospitals at least once a year. Nothing reconciles the unhappy to their lot but to see others suffer more, and to see what they themselves have escaped. The philosopher who suffers from *Taedium Vitae*, the fine lady who is *ennuyée,* the querulous, the discontented, should see the possibilities of suffering that are, alas! the inheritance of our race. Here, within earshot of the busy hum of city life, is a staid building. No pretence to architecture without; within, everything sacrificed to cleanliness and neatness. A few yards away, on the pavements of the great city, the votaries of Vanity are sweeping by, their little frames filled out and decorated with all the appliances that Art and Fashion can invent. They walk with the proud gait, the stately movements, of young gods and goddesses. The earth is theirs, and theirs is the heritage of the sky and sea. Here, ranged in long rows, are the couches of their suffering sisters. Very low and humble they are, as their breasts heave with the convulsions of difficult breathing, for that tiny occult mechanism has

22

built him a resting-place in their lungs, and is living by exhausting their life. Round, lustrous eyes, hectic cheeks, dry, hot hands, wet hair, are their sings and symbols, and creosote, formaldehyde, carbolic, have taken the place of the White Rose or Heliotrope which they shook from their raiment only a little while hence, as they spurned the very pavement beneath their feet.

Prisons and Asylums

Here, again, is another Temple of Hygeia, or rather of Death, for in these cancerous and tubercular cases the fair goddess is ruthlessly expelled by the skeleton god. Tossing on couches of pain, their entrails gnawed by the fell disease, or visibly rotting away from the malady in cheek, or tongue, or teeth, or breast, the poor victims linger on through a hell of agony, and invoke the King of Terrors in vain. And here is another Temple where some two thousand are lodged – beings once rational, but now with reason dethroned – helpless animals, ships without a rudder, tossed hither and thither through the stormy seas of their imaginings, with no power of guiding and directing themselves through the fierce impulses of animal instincts and desires. It is a cage for wild beasts. Witness the iron-barred windows, the padded cell, the various instruments of restraint, the strong men and women to cope with the paroxysms of insanity. And this is a Temple of Justice, wherein the elements dangerous to society are incarcerated. A thousand cells radiate from a central hall. In each is an outcast. Seated on a plank bed, staring at white-washed walls, fed like a beast through an aperture, each wretched soul ponders on his misery, eats his heart with remorse, or curses that society which, for is own safety and well-being, thinks it necessary to separate him from the rest of his fellow-mortals thus.

And so, side by side, the gay and the sorrowful, Fortune's darlings and Destiny's victims, move, in a kind of Holbein picture, towards the inevitable. Now, who hath cast the dice and appointed the lots of each? It is not merit, for in most cases my Lady of pain on her couch of suffering is a very much superior being to my Lady of pleasure on the pavement. But that is not the question now. The question now is, how can you repine at trifles, and fret yourself to death over imaginary troubles, like Molière's *Le Malade,* when you have escaped the coffin, the hospital, the gaol, the Bedlam, and all their terrible concomitants? And if you have come to middle age, or have mounted the mid-hill and crest of life, and are passing peacefully into the valley, how can you repine, when you have left so much misery behind you, and the fair vista of an honoured old age stretches before you? Oh, but that disappointment! That success of my neighbour's! That prosperous marriage! That successful speculation! He taken and I left! He with ten thousand a year, and I with only five! And he, with ten letters after his honoured name, and I with only six! Avaunt, thou ingrate! Thou who hast never proven –

How salt a savour hath
The bread of others, and how hard a path
To climb and to descend the stranger's stairs.

An Examination of Life

I would put side by side, in parallel columns with the Table of Sins in every Catholic prayer-book, an examination of escaped horrors thus: –

Hast thou ever been under the surgeon's knife? Hast thou ever seen the doctors in their white waterproofs, or bloodproofs, gaily chatting in the operation-room, and testing the edges of their knives, and thou on the table? Hast thou seen the sponges and the lint, and the splints, and the hot-water, and the nurses standing by the table, watching thee? Hast thou ever known the sickening odour of the anæsthetic, which is to send thee into the unknown bourn, from which thou mayest never return? Hast thou ever had sentence of death passed on thee by thy physician? That cough is phthisis; that little nodule of flesh is incipient cancer; that flush and chill is typhus; that sudden pain in thy left arm is cardiac trouble; that inability to grasp thy pen is incipient paralysis; that strange hesitation about thy words is brain disease. Hast thou ever dreaded the slow approach of insanity? Hast thou, like a certain great Cardinal, lived all thy life beneath its horrible shadow? Hast thou fallen into the grip of the law, and carried with thee the indelible stain of the prison? Nay, do not frown down the question as impertinent. Did not Philip Neri say to Philip, as he saw a criminal haled to execution: There thou goest, Philip, but for the grace of God! And if thou hast escaped all these things, and the many more too numerous to mention, go down on the knees, and thank thy God for His mercies!

The veil of Mercy

Thank God for the greatest mercy of all – that He has drawn down an impenetrable veil over thy future; and lifts the curtains of thy destiny, only fold by fold, and day by day. What would it be if the same Hand had unrolled for thee the map of thy life, and shown thee in thy adolescence all the terrors of thy future years? How thou wouldst have glided over the pleasures of thy existence with indifference, and fastened the eyes of thy imagination on the dangers and the pitfalls, the sorrows and the shames, that are marked so clearly on the diagram of thy existence! How thou wouldst extenuate and make little of life's pleasures; and ex- aggerate its pains! And with what terrible foreboding wouldst thou approach crisis after crisis in thy life; and forget the chance of victory in the dread of defeat! Verily, God is merciful! It is only to His great martyrs, most of all to the Queen of Martyrs, that he reveals the far-off Mount of Suffering; and allows the shadow of the three crosses cast by the setting sun of Olivet to darken the pathway of an entire life!

The ordering of destiny

I wonder is there a human being who would willingly take the ordering of his destiny out of the hands of Divine Providence, and cast the horoscope of his own life? Would he accept the proposal if made to him thus:

Now you can frame and form your future according to your own desires. You can have all that the human heart may desire – wealth, position, honours, influence, old age. But you must accept with them their concomitants; and the burden of your own imperfections. You can frame your future destiny; but you must bear it on your own shoulders; and look for no assistance from above.

No Christian believer would accept such a proposal; and it is doubtful even if a pure Agnostic would not shrink from the responsibility. We might elect to have the framing of our own futures, bit by bit; but to round our whole lives in the circle of our fantasies and wishes is a something we would shrink from. And then there is always the possibility of disappointment and defeat with the self-reproach that would accompany both if we made our own election. *Now,* if we fail, the failing is not of our own choosing. We can place it at the door of Destiny: or, with higher faith and meekness we can say it is the Will of God. But the sense of responsibility and remorse is absent, which would not be the case if disaster and defeat followed close in the wake of the voyage we had mapped for ourselves along the high seas of life. There! What a meditation I have made over an open trunk!!

26

The Lamp and the Firelight

Swish, swish, comes still the rain; but now it is night.
The short day has wept itself out; and its narrow twilight has yielded to great, black night. All the greater
security for you, my home-loving friend. It is dark at
four o'clock, and here are five long hours of uninterrupted, unbroken peace with your books and pen. How
the former glint and wink in the firelight and lamplight!
All day they were dull and silent. They seem to feel that
their time has now come, and they display all the finery
of bookbinding to attract attention. I can almost imagine
them saying, like the little children: 'Take me! Take me!'
and pouting, if left behind. Which shall I take? Well,
tastes vary. Sometimes, I take a violent fancy for biogra-
phies – the inner histories of remarkable men. I like to see
them turned inside out, and all their greatness and all
their weakness revealed. How imperative a thing was
genius! How it compelled work even to the starveling,
and compelled admiration even from the unwilling!
But, what an unhappy possession! If happiness were
the end and aim of existence, better be a hind than a
poet, 'a fool i' the forest' than a 'swan of Avon.' But this
is the unvarying equilibrium of life:

To learn in sorrow what they teach in song.

Travels

Sometimes, too, I put aside human lives, and wander
abroad on the wings of travellers, away to the South,
to the isles of the Mediterranean, bearing still on scarp
and cliff the ruins of the great Romans. Further still,
to the 'Isles of Greece,' haunted by all the melody of
the ancient language, and by the ghosts of all the singers
and heroes that are immortalized in verse, or statue, or
drama. Further still, to the silent monasteries of the
Levant, or the still more sequestered and archaic con-

vents there above the Ægean Sea. Further still, to the shores of Palestine – the sacred land – the home at Nazareth, where I should like to live forever – the cave at Bethlehem – the Sea, where Christ walked upon the waters, and to whose voluptuous cities, now crumbling ruins, He preached. Further still, to Egypt with all its mystic religions buried beneath its sands, and only the Eternal Sphinx looking out with its pathetic eyes for the reincarnation of its deities. Further still, to the lands of the Kaaba, and the Fire-worshippers, where the air is warm with hot scents above, and fetid with the germs of disease beneath near the surface. Further still, to the cradle of civilization, India, whence Aristotle drew his wisdom – the land of the Vishnu, and Siva, and Siddartha; of strange mysterious rites, where the natural fades away into the supernatural, and the visible calls to the unseen; the edge of the mysterious Orient, whence all faiths have come, to broaden out into mysticism and superstition, or to be concentrated into the vital and life-giving doctrines and ethics of Christianity.

Philosophers and Poets

But I have two constant, never varying loves – my philosophers and my poets. I cannot conceive a greater mental pleasure or stimulant than the study of mental philosophy. It is, after all, the *great* study. It is so clear, so defined, so perfect in definition and principle and axiom, that you feel quite safe and walking on level ground, until suddenly the great gulf yawns under your feet, and beneath you is roaring that unplummeted sea. You look down, down. It is crystal-clear, but no soundings. Here Plato gazed, and Aristotle pondered! Here Kant watched during his ninety years, only to turn away sadly in the end. Here, too, our child-philosophers of this unthinking age, fling their little lines weighted with modern discoveries. Alas! they will not even sink beneath the surface. And the great deeps are still unfathomed, and the great gulf unspanned. And yet the quest is not unfruitful. If it only taught humility, it would be a great gain. But it does more. It is like the vision of the Holy Grail that:

Drove them from all vainglories, rivalries,
And earthly heats that spring and sparkle out
Among us in the jousts, while women watch
Who wins, who falls; and waste the spiritual strength
Within us, better offered up to Heaven.

At least, we know of no dishonoured Knight of Philosophy. Votaries of other sciences may be impure. And alas! for our poets – the sacred fire does not always burn up carnal concupiscence. But Philosophy seems always to have kept her clients clean from grosser appetites and fleshly desires; and if they erred, it was through the spirit, and not through the flesh.

Macaulay

There is no author so worshipped by youth, so contemned by experience, as Lord Macaulay. I remember turning over and over like a delightful sweetmeat in the mouth those words of his:

It was a scene which Salvator would have loved to paint; and around which Claude Lorraine would have thrown all the glowing effulgence of the setting sun.

I had another melodious favourite from Telemaque:

Il me mena jusqu'au vaisseau; il demeura sur le rivage.

These were the happy days when we did not trouble much about sense, so long as we had sound. But in more mature years, the impertinent logic of common sense interferes, and tells us that there is colour-poison in that sweetmeat. In a word, that it is not true. And every Macaulayite must suffer disillusion. Nay, it seems really surprising that such an omnivorous reader should have committed himself to so many utterly untenable positions. Words came to him too easily, and he wrote too rapidly to be accurate. And then, – well, then, the public forgives a good deal to its favourites; and this he knew. But I think the most extravagant statement he made is that in his feeble essay on Lord Bacon, where he says: 'The ancient philosophy was a treadmill, not a path. It was a contrivance for having much exertion and no progress. Every trace of intellectual cultivation was there, except a harvest. There had been plenty of ploughing, harrowing, reaping, thrashing. But the garners contained only smut and stubble.' Macaulay does not conceal his sympathies with that purely utilitarian philosophy which places a shoemaker before a sage or a poet; and thinks the discovery of the powers of steam of far more importance than the institution of Christianity.

Utilitarianism

But is it not strange that, although the Baconian philosophy is justly credited with all these mechanical and material improvements that go to make what is called progress in our day, the world, which utilizes these improvements, persists in placing the leaders of purely metaphysical thought in kingly supremacy over all the race? Bacon himself descends to the rank of a second-rate philosopher, when placed side by side with a Hegel or a Fichte. No one would think of mentioning Stephenson in the same breath with Reid or Hamilton; or, in our own days, of placing an Edison or Marconi on the same level with Herbert Spencer or Lötze. Man's mind will ascend, in spite of material conveniences, far above purely physical and transitory things, and will busy itself for ever in seeking to measure space and infinity. And it is not on the crutches of the inventions of natural philosophy, but on the wings of speculative thought, it will ever seek to penetrate the unknown. All that human ingenuity can ever devise will never reach beyond the wings of Icarus. The soul's desires, passions, ambitions, reach higher. Mechanical inventions or discoveries, however ingenious and useful, can never become aught but toys in the hands of a Child of the Infinite. One thing alone lifts him into the empyrean, the elevation of pure thought, sublimated by faith, and raised by its power to regions otherwise impossible and inaccessible.

The Vision of Boëthius

All great writers have had their visions. 'In sleep, in a vision of the night,' revelations come. The Hebrew prophets stand out conspicuous by the multitude, the sublimity, or the horror of their dreams. Lucian seemed to have followed them, or imitated them. St. Augustine had his beautiful vision of Chastity, which left him in the agony of self-reproach, the prelude to his conversion. Every one knows the sublime picture of Philosophy drawn by the imagination of Boëthius:

While I was pondering this in silence, and using my pen to set down so tearful a complaint, there appeared standing over my head a woman's form, whose countenance was full of majesty, whose eyes shone as with fire, *and in powers of insight surpassed the eyes of men,* whose colour was full of life, whose strength was yet intact, though she was so full of years that none would ever think she was subject to such age as ours. One could but doubt her varying stature, for at one moment she repressed it to *the common measure of a man, at another she seemed to touch with her crown the very heavens*; and when she had raised higher her head, *it pierced even the sky,* and baffled the sight of those who would look upon it. Her clothing was wrought of the finest thread by subtle workmanship brought to an indivisible piece. This had she woven with her own hands, as I afterwards did learn by her own shewing. Their beauty was somewhat dimmed by the dulness of long neglect, as is seen in the smoke-grimed masks of our ancestors. On the border *below* was inwoven the symbol ,* *on that above* was to be read a .** And between the two letters there could be marked degrees, by which, as by the rungs of a ladder, ascent might be made from the *lower* principle to the *higher.* Yet the hands of rough men had torn this garment, and snatched such morsels as they could therefrom. In her right hand she carried books, in her left was a sceptre brandished.

Macaulay can hardly have seen this description, especially the lines we have ventured to italicise. But it is easy to understand how the Reformers esteemed as a compliment, as he tells us in that same essay on Lord Bacon, the reproach that was so fiercely levelled at them: 'Nullo apud Lutheranos philosophiam esse in pretio.'

Macaulay's Vision

Macaulay, too, had his vision, as he tells us in the least-known, yet, perhaps, the best of his poems. This, too, was in woman's form:

Oh, glorious lady, with the eyes of light,
    And laurels clustering round they lofty brow,
Who by the cradle's side didst watch that night,
    Warbling a sweet strange music, who wast thou?

The answer appears ambiguous; for no one seems able to decide whether it was philosophy or literature. But, evidence inclines somewhat to the former; and still more evidently to the former under any but a utilitarian aspect:

Without one envious sigh, one anxious scheme,
    The nether sphere, the fleeting hour resign;
Mine is the world of thought, the world of dream,
    Mine all the past; and all the future mine.

---

* *Πρακτική.*   ** *'θεωρητική.*

32

Fortune that lays in sport the mighty low,
    Age, that to penance turns the joys of youth,
Shall leave untouched the gifts that I bestow, –
    The sense of beauty, and the thirst of truth.

Of the fair brotherhood who share my grace,
    I, from thy natal day, pronounce thee free;
And if for some I keep a nobler place,
    I keep for none a happier than for thee.

This would seem to point to Literature as personified by
the Vision; for Macaulay did not lay claim to be considered a philosopher. Yet when she recalls her work, and
her protection of her votaries, one is insensibly reminded
of the figure that appeared to Boëthius:

In the dark hour of shame I deigned to stand
    Amid the frowning peers at Bacon's side;
On a far shore I smoothed with tender hand
    Through months of pain the sleepless bed of Hyde.

I brought the wise and great of ancient days
    To cheer the cell where Raleigh pined alone;
I lighted Milton's darkness with the blaze
    Of the bright ranks that guard the eternal throne.

Still more shall we give our vote for Philosophy, when
she makes her promises of protection and strength to her
client:

When friends turn pale, when envious traitors fly,
    When hard beset, thy spirit justly proud,
For truth, peace, freedom, mercy, dares defy
    A sullen faction, and a raving crowd.

Acid the din of all things, fell and vile,
    Hate's yell, and envy's hiss, and folly's bray,
Remember me; and with an unforced smile,
    See riches, baubles, flatterers, pass away.

The victim of Envy

So it would seem that Lord Macaulay, the most successful man of letters of his generation, did experience that
fine tonic of strong minds – the envy and jealousy of
his contemporaries. It is strange that this curious and
venomous antagonism does not seem to enter the sacred
precincts of Art, not yet the domain of Science. The
reason is evident. Only experts, who have passed through
a professional training will venture to criticise a picture,
or offer an opinion on a new discovery in Science. But in
literature, everyone is qualified to judge; and to reject
or accept, condemn or magnify a new appearance. Philosophy, however, has her atonements and consolations.
All will pass! It is the book-mark of St. Teresa over
again – honour, dishonour; the smile, the sneer; the
glory, the gibe; the laurel, the thorn; all will pass:

Yes, they will pass away; nor deem it strange;
   They come and go, as comes and goes the sea;
And let them come and go; thou through all change
   Fix thy firm gaz on Virtue and on me!

Night-watches

Some day, when science has made such advance that
human labour will be required no longer, men will sleep
by day, and watch the stars by night. For, of the two
revelations of Nature which strike the senses, unquestionably that of darkness is the more magnificent. We see
but one sun by day, and that a star of the second or third
magnitude; we see countless suns by night of every
colour and brilliancy. And scattered amongst them, here
and there, vast nebulæ, the seeds or laboratories of other
universes; and we know that creation and destruction,
the weaving of gases into suns, and the dissolution of
suns into gases; and the revolution of planets around
every sun; and the creation and conservation of vast
intelligences on each planet – that all these processes are

eternally going on, there in the workshop of the Eternal Mind, that stretches in its vast immensity through space, and is ubiquitous in its operations as well as infinite by its presence. What is the little work of our planet, lighted by one pale star, to this? What the birth of mere plants and flowers, the revolution of momentary seasons, the petty history of men, with their little wars and conquests, compared to the vast operations of the universe? You see littleness by day, greatness by night; limitations in the sunlight, infinity in the dark; man's little work by day, God's stupendous operations by night. And so, when we come to read more familiarly the book of the heavens and astronomy becomes a popular, from being an occult science, men will watch the stars all night; and derive from the evergrowing wonder and mystery of the Universe deeper veneration and greater love for the Mighty Spirit that rules and operates through all.

Divine darkness

Hence in the olden times when men thought much, and spoke little, they deemed the darkness divine. 'Ω τὸ θεῖον σκότος, 'O divine darkness!' said the Areopagite. 'Who hath made the darkness his hiding-place,' said the great thinker St. Paul, and there 'dwelleth in light inaccessible.' 'If you pierce this darkness,' said Nazianzen, 'who will flash forth?' Yes! darkness filleth space. Darkness is the ocean; the suns are but the lamps that float hither and thither on its surface. Consider only that immense field of utter and impenetrable darkness that stretches from the remotest orb of our solar system to the nearest fixed star! With the tremendous velocity of light − 186,000 miles in a second − it takes four hours to traverse our solar system, and reach its outer world, Neptune, or to bring back one ray to us from that remote and solitary world. But what is that to the awful chasm of darkness that lies beyond? For, from Neptune, a soul winged with the velocity of light would take not four minutes, but four years to reach the next sun and system!

What a black yawning immensity! What a universe of darkness! Looking back even from its threshold, our sun is but a glinting and flickering star; the planets are invisible. Very soon the sun itself dies out in the darkness, and all is night, night! Once and again in a century, perhaps, a mighty comet comes dashing out of space, as an express train would flash out of a tunnel, and swishes away with its long streamer of light into the darkness again. At intervals, there is a rumble or crash of the debris of worlds that broke up centuries ago. All else is midnight or gravelike blackness, until we break into the light of *Alpha Centauri,* and behold the sister-suns, for ever gravitating towards each other, and for ever kept apart by the Invisible Hand; and wheeling in circles of light around their resplendence, vast planets, drinking in life and beauty, and sweetness, form these glorious lamps in the streets of the Eternal City! And, away once through another ocean of darkness to the light of a more transcendent sun!

A Cataclysm

It struck me, one of those cold, frosty nights in late December, as I walked to and fro in my garden, and saw the surpassing splendours of the Winter's constellations, what a cataclysm there would be if that Infinite Hand were lifted for a moment from His Creation. No one, even the most sceptical, denies that Law, Supreme, Inexorable Law, guides and governs our Universe. But Law is merely another word for Will. So surely as the mariner's hand is on the helm of his ship, or the finger of the engineer is on the throttle of his express engine, so surely is the Hand of God upon the mighty mechanism of His Universe. Of course, worlds break up with their tremendous concussions, and scatter their fragments through space, to be resolved again into their original gases. Suns, too, are quenched, and their corresponding planets starved out of life, and frozen into lunar deserts. But this is only part and parcel of the Divine Economy, that builds out of ruin, and breaks only to reconstruct on a larger and greater plan. But let us suppose that a sun, like our own, could break from its moorings in space, and, taking the whole system with it, should plunge across the deserts of the universe, and carry its tremendous and liberated forces into the orbits of other suns and systems; and let us suppose that these, in turn, struck by this terrific and lawless energy, should be driven from their orbits, and carry their weight and velocities into the heart of other systems, until all were driven from their centres, where they had swung in perfect equilibrium, – what a fearful cataclysm it would be! What ruin upon ruin, destruction upon destruction would ensue! What conflagrations would light up the black deserts of interstellar spaces; and what glowing and incandescent gases, liberated by such gigantic convulsions, would stream across the universe! What awful thunders would shake the foundations of earth and rock the thrones of Heaven! And how all would finally settle down into primeval chaos, and darkness would fold its wings over a universe once more dissolved into atoms!

Man, the mystery

What a grotesque, beautiful, ridiculous, sublime little being is Man! Hanging on for a brief moment by the slender foothold he has on that little bubble in space, the Earth, he looks out from its darkened side into the Immensities that wheel above him; and he wants to understand them all, nay, to grasp them in his tiny fingers, and with his little mind. An insect looking out with wide, wondering eyes from an oak leaf in a forest, and feeling his way timorously with his antennæ, is not more insignificant. And yet this man is in reality *the* mystery of the Universe. For the latter is intelligible enough, and, to larger comprehensions, even simple in its greatness. And it is also demands God. He, too, is intelligible, because he is all greatness and sublimity. There is no need for reconcilements and adjustments there. All is simple; and all is great. But Man – 'Gentle-men,' said Fichte, in his introductory lecture on 'The Destination of Man,' in the University of Jena, 'collect yourselves – go into yourselves – for we have here noth-ing to do with things without, but simply with the inner self.' They drew themselves together. 'Gentlemen,' he continued, 'think the wall (*Denken Sie die Wand*).' They thought the wall. 'Now, gentlemen, think him who thought the wall.' Not so easy. There was evident em-barrassment. They shuffled in their seats. Some rose up. The wall was easy enough. They themselves were the mystery!

The Sphinx

Yes, say what we will, Man is the Mystery of Creation. God is no mystery to Himself, nor perhaps to the colossal intelligences that He has created. Nay, our own poor reason reaches to His existence at least. We see im-mensities and worlds, swimming in space; but see also order, law, everywhere. And we know there must be an Ordainer and a Legislator. And then we mount, step by step, to His ineffable attributes. It is only when we turn our eyes inward on ourselves, that we are smitten with astonishment. For, whereas all without us is cos-mical, uniform, perfect, all within us is chaotic and con-tradictory. We are a miracle and a mystery to our own comprehension. We know, but cannot tell why we know. Our senses are the sources or rather the conduits of knowledge, yet they deceive us. Our passions degrade us, or elevate us. To-day we grovel in the sty of Epicurus; to-morrow, our desires waft us into the empyrean. Our fellow-men are infinitely lovable, and infinitely hateful. Brute and angel, like the Woman-Beast that stares across the Egyptian sands, we watch for the reading of the riddle; but, unlike her, we cannot wait.

SECTION II.

De Quincey

One of the most repulsive things I ever read is de Quincey's description of the nebula of Orion. You will find it in his article on 'The System of the Heavens,' in Volume III. of his works. It is a fantasy, but an extremely morbid one. He sees in what is now recognized as one of the most beautiful objects in the heavens 'the horror of a regal phantasma which it has perfected to eyes of flesh.' 'All power being given to the awful enemy, he is beautiful where he pleases, in order to point and evenom his ghostly ugliness.' 'Brutalities unspeakable sit upon the upper lip, which is confluent with a snout; for separate nostrils there are none.' 'But the lower lip, which is drawn inwards with the curve of a marine shell – oh, what a convolute of cruelty and revenge is there! Cruelty! – to whom? Revenge! – for what? Pause not to ask; but loop upwards to other mysteries!' Probably, one of the greatest of these mysteries is, how the human mind could draw on the deep background of the infinities such a picture of horror and ugliness. It is the dream of one in delirium – the horrid spectre of a mind distorted by drugs, and weaving on the mirrors of infinite space the revolting pictures that are drawn on its own warped and twisted and shapeless faculties. True! It lasted only for a moment. The imagination gradually resolved itself into gentle and harmonious lines drawn by reason; and he says: 'He is now a vision to dream of, not to tell; he is ready for the worship of those that are tormented in sleep; and the stages of his solemn uncovering by astronomy are like the reversing of some heavenly doom, like the raising of one after another of the seals that had been sealed by the angel in the Revelation.'

The Constellations

What a contrast with the Greek mythology, pictured in the constellations! How these great artists, in the dawn of civilization, drew on the map of Night their own healthy dreams! If on their stages, they represented horror after horror, tragedy after tragedy, it was a kind of religious symbolism, marking the doctrine of Fate, and the steady Nemesis that follows upon and dogs the footsteps of crime; but, when they ascended on high, and drew on the heavens their symbols of immortality – the apotheoses of their heroes and their gods – they drew nothing revolting or inhuman or sanguinary; but wove the eternal stars into their legends of heroism and duty, and cast around the burning constellations a drapery of music, and painting, and sculpture, – put Cassiopeia on her throne, sent Perseus to rescue Andromeda, joined the Hunting Dogs in 'their leash of sidereal fire,' drew the imaginary chords of light across framework of Lyra, put a sword into the Hunter's hands, and swung another at his jewelled belt, and fretted the long filaments of light into the hair of the queen who sacrificed hers in the temple of Venus to ensure the return of her husband.

Opium-eating

There is no doubt that Greek thought was healthy thought. And health brought beauty; and beauty has brought immortality. How much of modern thought, especially of modern poetry, may be traced to the influences of opium, would be a nice question to determine. It seems that with many writers the brain will not work at its highest capacity, unless under the influence of the drug. Most of our modern writers have come under its spell. We owe some of the most spiritual and imaginative poetry to its inspiration. Some poets could never have touched the high altitudes they reached but for its help. Yet, the highest is not the healthiest, at least in common estimation. The human Shakspere is placed above the divine Dante, because he is human. There is something in the subject, as well as in its treatment. The sober Dante, intoxicated only by genius, ascended into the highest empyrean of human thought; the equally sober Shakspere touched ordinary humanity to transfigure it. But Coleridge could not have written the 'Ancient Mariner,' nor Shelley his marvellous 'Prometheus,' were not their imaginations excited by laudanum. Then, who shall say that the divine dreams come by inspiration, or who shall say the reverse? Or who shall mark the healthy from the morbid elements that go to compose the curious amalgam called Literature?

Richter

What a contrast between that morbid conception of a monster, cruel and merciless, into which the imagination of de Quincey turned the nebula of Orion, and the concluding passage from Richter, in the same essay! It is the voyage of a human being into the infinite.

'Suddenly, as thus they rode from infinite to infinite, suddenly, as thus they tilted over abysmal worlds, a mighty cry arose – that systems more mysterious, worlds more billowy – other heights, and other depths – were dawning, were nearing, were at hand. Then the man sighed, stopped, shuddered, and wept. His overladen heart uttered itself in tears, and he said: "Angel, I will go no further. For the spirit of man aches under this infinity. Insufferable is the glory of God's house. Let me lie down in the grave, that I may find rest from the persecutions of the Infinite; for end, I see, there is none." And from all the listening stars that shone around issued one choral chant – "Even so it is; angel, thou knowest that it is; end there is none, that ever yet we heard of." "End is there none?" the angel solemnly demanded. "And is this the sorrow that kills you?" But no voice answered, that he might answer himself. Then the angel threw up his glorious hands to the heaven of heavens, saying: "End is there none to the universe of God? Lo! also there is no beginning."'

There is a deep and solemn truth in that line: 'The spirit of man aches under infinity!' He is not equal to it. Its vastness weighs upon him like a thick atmosphere on feeble lungs. Like one, lost in a desert, the solitude appals him, and he cries aloud for help, for companionship.

Aching under Infinity

Yet, what a wayward being he is! All his aspirations are towards the infinite that oppresses him. He loathes his prison – the earth; he despises his fellow-prisoners. Humanity is beneath him; the earth is too small to bear him. Looking through the bars of his prison-house, across the levels of twilight seas, he yearns to go out and be lost in the sun-mists that gather away on the horizon; and if a faint sail shimmers on the line of the sky and sea, it is to him the burden, and the jealous burden of a soul, that, emancipated, is pursuing its happy way to the Infinite. So, too, does he dream in mountain solitudes, looking up from vale to peak, and from peak to cloud, happy in the thought that some day he may go thither, unhappy in the reflection that 'his sojourning is prolonged.' Yet, give him this infinity whilst still in the flesh, and lo! he 'aches under it.' He tires of stars and systems. His wonder ceases when his imagination is satiated. Knowledge destroys the magic of the Universe. The wilderness of galaxies becomes an unpeopled solitude. He is perishing amidst the splendours of space. He cries aloud in his agony. He wants the earth, and men!

The Earth, man's home

Yes! till disembodied, earth is his home – the little theatre of his sufferings and joys. Here he is placed by the Omnipotent; and here he has to accomplish his destiny. He is finite and must take his limitations. His wings will not bear him far towards the Infinite. They grow weary and droop, and he falls. Yes! here on this little planet are his destinies environed by time and space. Here shall he find the little loves, the little cares, the little worries, the little joys, that make up his daily experience. However high he soars in the empyrean, a line draws him back to earth. He is an imprisoned immortal. He is created for the Infinite, but not permitted to seek his place as yet. That will come. Meanwhile, let him dream and aspire, for that is good, and reminds him that here he hath no lasting habitation. But he must not despise the little part he has to play on this planet, nor must he segregate himself too much from sympathies with his own feeble and much-complaining race. And there two watchwords to inspire him – one, the password of the nightwatch – Duty! and one, the password of the relief at dawn; and that is Destiny!

Knowledge begets contempt

And yet, what an insolent and insatiable little parasite he is! Knowledge begets wonder; and wonder gives way to contempt. Tell him all the fairy tales of science; and his open, round eyes stare at you, first in incredulity, and then surprise. Tell him that the Demon-star, Algol, is twice as large as our sun; that its dark satellite, moving only 3,000,000 miles apart, is the same size as our sun, with a density one-fourth as great; that this satellite extinguishes its own luminary for us for a space of twenty minutes every two days and ten hours – he stands still in surprise, stares at the celestial prodigy, weighs it in his own mind, until this latter growing under the exercise, first equals, then surpasses the limits of the wonderful; and then passing far beyond it, looks on it with a certain contempt. Or, tell him the two component stars of Mizar are forty times as great as the mass of our sun, 150,000,000 miles apart from each other, and moving with a velocity of fifty miles a second; his little mind strives to battle with these stupendous figures, then seizes them and holds them; then in its marvellous elasticity surrounds them and encompasses them in the net of his own imagination; finally, goes so far beyond them that it regards them as infinitesimal accidents in space. Nay, you cannot tire it, nor exhaust it. The circumference of human thought is conterminous with the horizon of space!

The Infinite Void

What then does Richter mean, when he speaks of the soul 'aching' under the Infinite? Clearly, he means the Infinite Void – the Material Infinite! It is the hollow eye of Infinity, bare of God, that glares on him and terrifies him. The sense of infinite solitude becomes unbearable – such solitude as oppresses the mind when one stands beneath the crater of Vesuvius, knee-deep in hot ashes, and sees above him a canopy of fire, and all around the horrors of utter desolation. Viewed thus, creation becomes simply a universe of volcanic forces, pitched and heaved, hither and thither in endless chaos, the little planetary worlds with their tiny and solitary sweetnesses, insignificant oases in the deserts of infinity. It was such a vision as the fiend saw, when Sin opened the eternal gates: –

Before their eyes in sudden view appear
The secrets of the hoary deep, a dark
Illimitable ocean, without bound,
Without dimension, where length, breadth and heigth,
And time and place are lost; where oldest Night,
And Chaos, ancestors of Nature, hold
Eternal anarchy amidst the noise
Of endless wars and by confusion stand,

In this 'vast vacuity,' this 'womb of Nature, and perhaps her grave,' man's spirit faints away. The senses of sight and hearing are smitten with the tumult and din of worlds hustling through unlighted space. He sinks down, and cries: 'Father, where art Thou!'

44

The Immensity of God

Why, then, is the little being so impatient of his lot, so eager for the Infinite? Because it is not the infinity of emptiness, but the immensity of God he his unconsciously seeking. It is not the Universe he wants, but the God of the Universe. The end and term of his existence found, he seeks no more. He no longer aches under infinity, but basks in its immensities. He no longer dreads the hollow eye of Nature, because he knows the eye of the Father is upon him; he no longer dreads the awful mechanism around him, because he knows he is in the workshop of his Friend. And the vast deserts of the Universe are closed to his sight by the

... empyrean Heaven, extended wide,
In circuit, undetermined square or round,
With opal towers and battlements adorned,
Of living sapphire, once his native seat:

and

... the Almighty Father from above
From the pure empyrean where He sits,
High throned above all height, bends down His eye
His own works and their works at once to view.
About Him all the sanctities of heaven
Stand thick as stars, and from His sight receive
Beatitude past utterance.

St. Augustine and Maine de Biran

I dare say this idea of the limitation of human action and feeling, and the eternal craving after the infinite and illimitable in the human mind, can be seen exemplified in most human lives. Especially is it observable in men of thought or fine sensibilities. But I have seen it confessed clearly only in two lives, that of St. Augustine, as revealed in his *Confessions;* and that of Maine de Biran, as revealed in his *Thoughts*. The latter was one of those unhappy immortals who, to their own sorrow, but the everlasting benefit of mankind, have been tortured by nerves. He was so finely constructed that his emotions swayed to the slightest touch, swinging low down in the deepest depression at a word or look, or a reverse or a dyspepsia, and again thrown into the empyrean of exalted reflection by equally minute and trifling causes. These *Pensées* would be pitiful reading were they not relieved here and there by gleams of inspiration – great lightning-flashes of thought athwart the low thunder clouds of despondency. His life was an alternation of desires for solitude when in society, and impatience of self when in solitude. 'La commerce des hommes,' he writes, 'm'a gâté et me gâte tous les jours;' but he was for ever craving for their companionship amongst the woods and waters of Grateloup. 'I walk like a somnambulist in the world of affairs.' But when it came to the point to choose, he refused to say the word, and turned back to politics. He is a stranger amidst the pomps and ceremonies of the French Court; he hates himself for his presence there and his nervous unsuitableness; but he cannot remain away. He clamours for the infinity of thought in solitude, but craves for the limitations of action in society.

La Soif de Dieu

Very early in life, and long before he became a Christian in thought and feeling, he recognised the composite nature in man, and writes strongly against Voltaire and Condillac, and all the tribe of writers of the sensist or materialist school. He will not admit the sovereignty of sense; he demands the supremacy of the soul. But does he find peace, the peace for which he is for ever clamouring? He admits it is the *summum bonum*, nay, the only good here below. He confesses his contempt for the things which the world prizes. He has seen them, and tested their hollowness. He flies from them and buries himself in the desert of his own soul. The philosophy of the Porch is now his religion. He will be self-sufficing. He will subdue all riotous feeling of passion, and even sensation, and under the arbitrary rule of the soul he will find peace. He will desire nothing, and therefore want nothing. All shall be harmony of nicely adjusted thoughts and sentiments, of passions subdued and reined by a strong hand; Nature shall yield its manifold treasures of peaceful bliss; and an imagination, rightly controlled, will serve to lift the soul beyond time and death, and project another existence on the canvass of eternity. But the oaks and streams heard still but the agony of a disappointed and despairing soul. Yes! all was satisfied, but the insatiable – *La Soif de Dieu!*

Solitude

He liked, as all such souls like, every line that speaks of the beauty and happiness of a solitary life. And all literature, Divine and human, is replete with those threnodies of the heart – the desire to be away, and at rest. 'Would that I had the wings of a dove;' 'O for a lodge in some vast wilderness!' Was the author of the *Imitation* merely parodying the words of St. Augustine in all the many curious ways he had of uttering the same thought: *Noli foras abire; in teipsum redi; in interiore homine habitat veritas*? And I suppose most people (always excepting the artists themselves) must have felt a little *attendrissement du cœur* at the closing lines of that favorite duet in *Trovatore:* 'There shall be rest! there shall be rest!' Certain it is that Maine de Biran was forever craving rest, rest – from the fever of fashion, from the turmoil of politics, from the stings of wasps, the hollowness and insincerity of the world; and he was for ever dreaming in the Court of Versailles or at the Tuileries of his woods and walks, of the rustling leaves, the singing of birds, the purling of streams, the peace of the mountains, the solitude of the peace of the mountains, the solitude of the valleys. Then came the reality. Lo! here is all this sylvan beauty; and here is solitude deep enough for a Bruno! And here is peace, and deep profound thought, and the absorption of the soul in the reveries of metaphysics. Alas, no! or not altogether. A cloudy sky, an indiscretion at table, a look, a word; and lo! the paradise is broken up. So dependent is the soul on the caprices of the body! There are two principles in man – *et primum quod est animale!*

The equilibrium of things

'Bene qui latuit, bene vixit!' It was a favourite maxim of Descartes who had also another favourite doctrine, which I recommend earnestly, namely, the sanitary value to mind and body, of long fits of idleness. Maine de Biran would not, and did not, accept the latter. He could not. He was made otherwise, a thing compacted out of nerves, and fed by a planet and a star – by Mercury and Phosphor. He knew well the glorious blessing of such a constitution, and – its curse. He admits that the dull, practical, geometrical reasoner has less joy out of youth, but more security in age. And that if the nervous dreamer and thinker has visions of the gods in his heyday, he must suffer by diabolic apparitions in the evening of his days. It is the eternal equilibrium of things – the just apportionment of fate to mortals. The most careful chemist does not sift and mix on his glass measure the drugs that make for life or death so carefully as the Fates dole out their destinies to mortals. Or, rather, not *destinies,* but the factors of destinies – the powers of action or suffering, of reason and imagination, of mental or physical constituents, that go to construct the sum total of those transient dreams or experiences which we call Life.

Un philosophe manqué

But the maxim of Descartes: 'Bene qui latuit, bene vixit!' he loved it, but did not accept it. Or rather, accepted it only in theory. It is the motto of those who are surfeited by fame, or notoriety; not of those who have never tasted either. Men can despise riches when they possess them; fame, when the wicked goddless woos them. But all men would like to drink from the cup of Tantalus, and grasp the skirts of the phantom, Fame. Yet, Maine de Biran, let it be said, had even a nobler ambition. He deplores the necessity of his taking part in political and social matters to the exclusion of intellectual pursuits, for which he believed he possessed a certain aptitude. And life was passing by; and nothing done. All this externation which he detested, but which arrested every movement towards the life of solitude and retreat which he coveted, induced at last a condition of intellectual atrophy from want of exercise; and he saw himself far advanced into middle age, without the prospect or hope of realizing his own ambition – 'avoir laissé quelque monument honorable de son passage sur la terre.' A victim of circumstances, a prey to ill-health, with all the power and the desire of becoming the foremost thinker of his age, he remained to the end – *un philosophe manqué.*

The Abstract and the Concrete

It is quite clear that thought and existence are not identical; and that each must have its own rules, aspirations, conditions. For example, the illimitable sea at sunset, with just one solitary sail on its way to infinity, fills us with the strongest emotions. We can gaze and gaze at it for ever. It is a soul, emancipated, and passing out on its voyage to the unknown eternities. But, lo! some one says: Beneath that line is the coast of France; and that schooner is bound for Cherbourg! The spell is broken! Why? Because the abstract, the illimitable, is suddenly bounded by the concrete and determined; and the soul beats itself against that rude and imperious barrier. Or we watch the heavy rain-clouds, these winter evenings, driven up and on by the south-west wind. Their gloomy

battalions file over our heads, black and threatening, like
the remnants of a conquered army, driven on before the
exultant conquerors. We can see them, with some pleasure, drifting, drifting towards the unseen north-east. It
is an undefined, an abstract destination. But, let some
one say: The clouds are drifting over such and such a
mountain; they are now above such a town, now over
such a village. Again the spell is broken. We don't care
to watch them any longer. They are no longer creatures
of the infinite. We see them swoop down, and draw their
wet skirts across the mountain heather, or the roofs of
houses, and then vanish in mere rain and storm.

The worship of silence

What is the fittest form of worship in the temple of the
Eternal, under that awful dome of blackness that leans
on the horizons of infinity? If we consider for a moment
the total want of proportion between our weak praise
and the immensity of God, we are tempted to take refuge
with the mystics, and say, *Silentium sit laus!* St. Augustine seems to have felt most intensely this utter inade-
quacy of man to sing worthily the praises of God. 'When
the Psalmist cried out, *"Magnus Dominus et laudabilis
nimis quoniam magnitudinis ejus non est finis,"* he
wanted to show,' says St. Augustine, 'how great He is.
But how can this be done? Though he repeated, *great,
great,* the whole day, it would have been to no purpose,
because he must have ended at last, for the day must be
ended. But His greatness was before the beginning of
days, and will reach beyond the end of time.' So, too,
says that wonderful old poet-saint, Synesius, of whom
we know but too little:

> Ὑμνῶ σέ, Μάκαρ,
> Καὶ διά φωνᾶς.
> Ὑμνῶ σέ, Μάκαρ,
> Καὶ διά σιγᾶς.
> Ὅσα γὰρ φωνᾶς,

Τόσα καὶ σιγᾷς,
Ἄιεις νοεράς,
Πάτερ ἄγνωστε,
Πάτερ ἄρρητε.*

Whilst all this is true, it is also true that we need a language of praise. Does not the Evangelist place the very words in the mouths of the Seraphim, by which they may glorify God?

The worship of the Psalms

And what more worthy language ever was, or could be, invented for this sacred purpose than the Psalms of David? I have an idea that our piety, as Catholics, would be more robust, and that we would be brought more close to God, if the inspired words, the language of the Holy Spirit, formed a larger portion of our daily prayers. We have many and excellent books of devotion; but after all they are compiled by men, and breathe but a human language. But the words of Scripture are the words of the Holy Spirit; and they are winged with the fiery tongues of the Paraclete. Could there be for example, a more perfect act of charity than the seventeenth Psalm, *Diligam te, Domine*, with the sublime poetry of the verses 8-17; or a more piteous appeal for mercy than Psalm 21, *Deus, Deus meus, respice in me*, with all its pathetic foreshadowing of the Passion; or a more glorious bit of

* All-Holy, I hymn Thee
  Even with my voice.
  All-Holy, I hymn Thee
  Even in silence.
  Whatever the voice
  Uttereth, the silence
  Equally speaketh.
  Yea, silence alone
  Seems worthy of Thee.
  Father, unspeakable!
  Father, unknown!

nature-painting than Psalm 103, *Benedic, anima mea, Dominum;* or lastly, a more tender and more childlike profession of faith and obedience than Psalm 118, which is so familiar to us in the daily Office, and which I had marked twenty golden years ago in my Douay Bible as *Pascal's Psalm?*

God is Light

That is a fine expression of Plato's, *Lux est umbra Dei.* Light is the shadow of God. *Et Deus est Lumen Luminis.* And God is the Light of Light. How closely his language approaches the words of the Nicene Creed! Could they have been adapted from him by those Oriental Fathers? The idea runs through the whole of the inspired writings. 'He dwelleth in light inaccessible.' 'Erat lux vera.' And the 'Lamb was the lamp thereof.' Yet we read that He is surrounded by darkness. 'He bound the heavens and came down; and darkness was under His feet. And He made darkness His covert; His pavilion round about Him; dark waters in the clouds of the air.' This, and other figurative language would seem to convey the idea that God, the Light, is hidden away in His creation, not like a far sun localized in a defined space of darkness, but permeating as a hidden force all space and all darkness, as lightning is concealed in the dark folds of a cloud. And, as lightning is hardly seen in light, but illumines a whole world in the darkness of night; so it is at night, God's illumination breaks upon the soul of man, and he feels all around him the presence of the Divinity.

The revelations of darkness

For, it was really a happy thought of that mediæval writer,* who wrote so little but so well, that it is dark-

* Sir Thomas Browne.

ness that reveals to us the universe. If there were no
night, but perpetual day, man could never have reached
a conception of the immensity and grandeur of the
heavens. We should see the blue vault of heaven without
knowing it was a sea of darkness in which the lightships
of God floated. We should know our sun, and have a
dim idea of the moon as a bright silver cloud, but no
more. Lo! darkness envelops the earth, and reveals the
heavens. Here, from his lonely watchtower, the eye
of the little creature takes in all the vastness and sublimity that lie around him; he sees himself on the lonely
deck of a little ship in space. He knows his insignificance
and God's greatness, and he is humble. Lo! once more
come the dawn and the light. The curtains of the night
are drawn; immensity vanishes; the tiny ark of humanity
swells to a vast world where he is king and master. And
all the vast deceptions of life, which had faded before
infinity, throng around him once more to cheat his
senses and flatter his pride. The ghosts do not vanish
at dawn; they are the creatures, not of darkness, but of
light.

Night-thoughts, deepest

Hence, I suppose, that saying of Euripedes: βαθύτεραι
γὰρ νυκτὸς φρένες.   Night-thoughts are deepest. The
sense of immensity, the darkness, shutting out all those
myriad sensible objects that fret and distract the mind,
the silence, always unbroken except by soothing sounds
of winds or waterfalls – all these help to cast back the
mind upon itself, and by concentrating its faculties, to
intensify thought and subdue emotion. Could this be the
reason, apart from the leisure it afforded, why the Son
of God found strength and respite by spending the night
in prayer in the solitude of the mountains? This was
foreshadowed, as the Psalmist foreshadowed the Divine
Being Himself, by the midnight prayer of David. *Media
nocte surgebam ad confitendum tibi.* And all the saints
have loved the night-prayer. There is no hour so dear to

them as the Matin-hour, which is in deepest darkness as it precedes the dawn. And is it not proverbial that scholars love the time of night-thoughts; and that 'burning the midnight oil' has passed into a metaphor for lonely studies at the deepest part of the night? Yes, we want solitude to think deeply, and 'night uttereth knowledge to night' in other senses than the Psalmist meant.

Sense and Sound

If all knowledge comes through the senses, that knowledge must be necessarily limited, four our senses are very weak. The lower animals possess senses far more acute than ours, as their anticipations of atmospheric changes clearly demonstrate. Nay, even, they seem to be able to forecast great cataclysms on earth, as they manifest signs of perturbation and fear before earthquakes or volcanic eruptions, where man sees no cause for alarm. The sense of hearing with us seems the dullest of the senses. We feel the heat of the sun, and rejoice in his light. But what of the tremendous reverberations and thunders that are forever flung into space from the convulsions of that mighty furnace? Not a sound reaches us. Here, to all outward seeming, is a meek sun, shedding beneficent heat and light on his satellites, and silently performing his allotted duty in the Universe. But reason will not tolerate this assumption. It argues that if a tiny black cloud, perched half a mile above the earth, can vomit flame and thunder, so as to drown the loudest noises on earth, what an unimaginable tumult of sound breaks from that fiery furnace, which flings out its waves of flame a quarter of a million miles beyond its surface. Now, wherefore this waste? The heat and light of the sun are not scattered objectless through space. Why should sound? Or, has it a purpose in Nature, which, though it never reaches us, is nevertheless accomplished?

The choral anthem of the Universe

It is really difficult for us to get rid of the idea that this little planet of ours is the centre of the Universe, that all space revolves around it as on a pivot, and that all things in heaven and on earth were made for man. Our pride is always striving to disprove what reason and science assert. Yet we shall never understand things until we get outside ourselves; nor shall we ever grasp the secret of the Universe until we begin to acknowledge the weakness of our understanding. 'My thoughts are not as your thoughts,' said the Lord; 'nor My ways as your ways.' All that science, with its Argus eyes, has hitherto testified is this: Space is a universe of darkness, and the murk of midnight, and cold, pierced here and there by suns, which, though to our imaginations they are colossal and gigantic, are nevertheless pinpoints of light in the vast deserts around them. These lamps in the midnight are surrounded by tiny moths of planets, that are forever seeking to destroy themselves in the flame, but are kept apart by an unseen Hand. And that is all. Yes, all to the limited faculties and purblind sight of this little parasite called man. But what if that desert of darkness were transcendent light to other eyes than ours; and what if outside our limited cognizance, the vast regions of space were all light and no darkness; and what if the irregular patches of constellations stretched themselves, in obedience to the eternal law of cosmical symmetry and beauty, into a great line of light, sentinelling the outher darkness of our space, and forming a mighty cordon around the white central throne; and what if, after all, 'the music of the spheres' and 'stars quiring to the young-eyed Cherubim' were more than poetic fancies, and that, in fact, the whole Universe is eternally resonant with praise; and that the tumultuous thunders of countless suns and worlds are toned down into the organ accompaniment of the Hosannas that echo forever, and forever and ever, around the great Throne of God! Clearly, there is nothing for us, little ephemeræ as we are, but to sit still, and see the salvation of God!

God is a Spirit

But there is one thought that continually obtrudes itself on your waking senses at night – *God is a Spirit*. It is an idea that is too seldom before us as a subject for meditation. It is one of those sublime truths that, with all their meaning, flash suddenly upon our intellects, and bewilder them. The fact is, we seldom see truths in their entirety. Each has as many facets as a crystal; and now we see one; now, another. There are some truths whose farthest side we never see, as we never see the far face of the moon. But we are so dazed and bewildered by sensible objects that, daily and momentarily, strike our senses, that the idea of God as a Spiritual Essence or Being is unfamiliar to us. We always represent Him to the imagination as a human being – old, venerable, kind – yet a man, and therefore limited and imperfect. Now, this is not an adequate conception of God. But can we form an adequate conception? No. But we may form a worthy conception, worthy of us, if not of Him; and this we cannot do, unless we strive to understand those words of our Lord: God is a Spirit!

Our idea of spirit

But how can we form an idea of a spirit? Is not this impossible in our condition of being? It is not. We cannot paint a spirit, nor describe it, except in human terms. But we may conceive it, or at least those abstract qualities which we associate with it. The thought, for example, that we are surrounded by God, as a fish by the sea, as a bird by the air, that he is closer to us than breathing, nearer than hands or feet, conveys an idea of omnipresence, which we could never understand if He were represented under a merely human form. Then the idea that He is a spirit, endowed with subtlety, immensity, penetration, leads us to understand His omnipotence far better than a representation of hands and feet; and, lastly, when we combine with that idea the final perfection of goodness and love, we come to feel that in us, around us, above us, is that mysterious entity, invisible intangible, in whose embraces we float, in whose arms we rest, secure in the double conviction that here are the two faculties which assure our safety, here and hereafter – merciful omnipotence and all-powerful love.

Representations of God

I do not find fault with painters and artists who strive to draw on canvas their conceptions of Deity. They cannot do better. They must rise above mere symbolic representations. The Eye in a Triangle, the Circle with wings of light, are very feeble embodiments of God. Nothing then is left but the representation of God as the *Pater Aeternus, Creator coeli et terrae.* But this corporeal representation excludes the idea of spirit, although otherwise meant. And they, who never lift their eyes beyond that symbol of paternity, and never try to see the spirituality of God, fail to surround their imaginations with the loftiest conceptions of that transcendent Being, who, in using human language to express His manifold perfections, could only say, I AM WHO AM. But it seems that there was at least some special significance in that saying of our Lord's: *Deus est spiritus;* for the word 'spirit' in Hebrew, Greek, and other languages signifies a gentle gale of wind; and as this surrounds us, wraps us all around, penetrates us, soothes us, compels us, refreshes us, though we neither see it, nor know whence it has come, or whither it goeth, so with that ineffable Being, in whom 'we live, and move, and are.'

Our Guardian Angels

The sense of the presence of a guardian-Angel a dear, familiar spirit, dividing with his care for us the blisses of Heaven, to be the companion of our mortal pilgrimage, is very soothing and strengthening. One comes to love that unseen being, ever at our side, watchful, zealous, merciful, loving protecting. But it is his very unseenness that makes us love him; and also the sense of our dependence. For if the sense of protection is the secret of maternal and other perfect, unselfish love, on the other hand the feeling of weakness and dependence constitutes filial affection. But, let us expand even to infinity the attributes of our Angel; let us see him as a speck in a sea of light; let us know that he, too, is dependent on the Supreme; and then, let us add up, in the feeble arithmetic of reason, all that we know of fine spiritualities, their unearthiliness, their purity, their unselfishness, their power, their love, and then multiply this sum of all inconceivable excellence by the vast cyphers of infinity; and we shall have an idea of that transcendent Being, who filleth the desert of the Universe, and lightens their loneliness with His Infinite Beauty; and in whose embraces we, the least ones of His intelligent creation, repose in security and peace, whilst He veils His splendours from us.

> Ὅς πάντα πληροῖ, καὶ ἄνω παντὸς μένει.
> Ὅς νοῦν σοφίζει, καὶ νόου φεύγει βολάς.

Who filleth all things, yet abideth above all;
Who giveth wisdom to the mind yet fleeth all scrutiny.

The Incarnation

And yet this will not do for all persons, at all times. The soul faints in contemplating God as a Spirit. It needs the visible, the tangible. Hence the Incarnation, if it were not necessary, would be inevitable. Hence, too, the absolute necessity of the Real Presence, if faith and love were to be preserved amongst men. The Israelites of old needed the perpetual monitions of God to keep alive their feeble, intermittent faith. Nay, with all the terrible reminders of His presence, how frequently and

58

how foully they fell! Under the very shadow of the clouded mountain, and with its thunders pealing above their heads, they fell into the basest idolatry. We cannot boast that we are of stronger fibre than they. How then could God substitute a Book for His Presence? The New Laws was to perfect the Old. If so, God must have come nearer to His people. The cloud vanished; the pillar of fire disappeared; the ark was destroyed. But where was God? Nearer in His personal presence. Certainly. This was inevitable. If Jehovah vanished, it was to leave a closer and nearer substitute of His presence. But how? As a Spirit? No! This would have been as far from the craving sense of men as the God of the Deluge, or Sinai. How then could He come nearer to men, nearer to their senses, as well as to their faith? Only in one way. *Verbum Caro factum est; et vidimus gloriam ejus, gloriam quasi Unigeniti a Patre, plenum gratiae et veritatis.*

The New Law and the Old

The New Law would be more imperfect than the Old, if God did not come closer to His people. But this could only be accomplished by His visible presence. But there could be no visible presence of God, but as Man. God should therefore become Man to reveal Himself fully to the world. This He did in His incarnation. But again it was quite clear He could not remain forever visibly amongst us. On the other hand, a merely historical Christ would have left the work of union and revelation imperfect. A book is no substitute for a Being, especially when that Being is God. To complete the whole scheme of Divine economy, therefore, the presence of God should be maintained. Otherwise, the Christian would have been of less consequence that the Israelite, to whom Jehovah spoke and manifested His presence. But how could the presence of God become a lasting memorial of His love, and yet be veiled in such shadows and accidents that man should have perfect faith, yet not be 'overwhelmed with glory'? Only in one way – the only possible way consistent with the dignity of the Most-High – the way His Divine ingenuity discovered for the most stupendous mystery He has wrought – namely, the entombment of the Ever Living and Eternal under the lowliest and most perishable of elements in the ineffable Sacrament of the Altar.

Carlyle and the Mass

Carlyle, in his extreme old age, and when every vestige of faith or religious credence had left him, admitted to his biographer, Froude, that the Mass was the only relic of religious faith now left in the world. It was a curious and even valuable admission. He had no love for Catholicity. The old spirit of Calvinism, in which he had been reared survived under the dark gloomy philosophy he had tried to place in its stead; and there is no heresy so antagonistic to the brightness and beauty of Catholic Doctrine as Calvinism. But the old sage had read and thought and seen much; and even in the pale light of history, he had observed the great fact, that the sacrifice of the upper-room in Jerusalem, and of Calvary, the sacrifice of the Catacombs and the Deserts, was perpetuated through all the succeeding ages of the Church's history; and was now, what it always has been, the great fact in the ever varying history of mankind. And so, too, if ever the day should come when civil holidays will completely usurp the place of Saints' holidays, the world will hesitate, again and again, before it removes the great festival of 'Christ's Mass' from the calendars of men.

Christmas

It comes as a sudden sun in the darkness of mid-winter. Its illumination, as of hope, stretches far back into the gloom of November; and far forward as a memory, into the cold and storms of January. Weary men look to it as a time of armistice or truce, when they may forget they are enemies, and believe they are friends and brothers. For, alas! that it should be true, all men accept the verdict of the stricken Job, and believe that life is a warfare; and most men think themselves Ishmaelites, with the hands of the rest of mankind against them. They do not like it – this struggle for the survival of the fittest. It is hard, scientific, brutal. But so they are taught; and so they learn all too aptly. They would fain unlace their helmets, and unbuckle their armour, and unloose their greaves; and lie down by the common stream to drink and repose, before taking up their weapons again. Well, Christmas is just such a time. The little Child suddenly appears; and contention is hushed. Humanity asserts itself in Him who assumed it, and all the belligerents bow down. Courtesies are interchanged; the finer feelings come uppermost; men grasp one another's hands in friendship. They think of the fallen – the dead. They touch the fingers of those who are far off. They allow a tear to gather and fall. It is well! Soon must they take up their weapons and go forth; and steel their hearts against the finer thoughts, that still remain to humanize them.

The warriors and the Child

If I mistake not, some such instance of sudden pause and human awakening occurred in the Civil War. Two detachments of Union and Confederate troops had been watching each other for days seeking the hour for the successful destruction of the enemy. At last they came into touch with each other. The scouts announced their proximity. There was a river and a bridge between them; and the great objective on either side was the capture and retention of that bridge. Both pushed forward, reconnoitred, charged. Just as they gained the entrance on either side, the foremost troops checked their horses, and pressed back their comrades to a sudden halt. For right in their track, on the roadway, was a child of two summers. It was playing with flowers, with all the delightful innocence and unconsciousness of childhood. It knew nothing of its peril. 'It feared no danger, for it knew no sin.' Then it saw the advancing troopers, who had slowed down to a walk. Its eye caught their splendid uniforms and the trappings of their horses, and it smiled. The foremost dragoon leaned down, and picking up the waif, placed it on the pommel of his saddle. Friends and enemies gathered around, and sought its smiles. It was a pause of pity in the game of destruction. Men wondered at one another, and grew ashamed, and smiled. Gloved hands met, and scabbard made music with scabbard. Then they parted, and went their several ways once more. It was Christmas, and the Christ!

Life a hymn

Where do the words occur: *La vie est un combat pas un hymne*. Yes! but is this the design of the Creator; or rather the serult of man's own perversity? But, admitting that life must be a warfare, why should not a hymn mingle with the clash of arms and even drown it? Not a hymn over the fallen – a hymn of triumph over defeat and death; but a hymn of praise to the Lord of Battles for the peace His wisdom has imparted to ourselves. And is not this duty of praise, this obligation of worship and stealing the 'Sanctus' from the lips of Archangels, the one duty which we, through false humility, or selfishness, neglect? We pour out our painful *Misereres* in the ear of Heaven. Why should not an exultant *Magnificat* occasionally rise above them, if it were only to prove to Heaven that we are not altogether mendicants, but mindful of our eternal destiny to take our places on the thrones vacated by the spirits who forgot their obligations of praise in the paroxysms of pride? What is the hymnology of the Church for, if it be not to put the canticles of joy and praise upon our lips? Let us have our days of weeping and our places of mourning, if you like, as the Jews down there in the Valley of Hinnom,

62

with their faces against the foundations of the temple that shall never be rebuilt. But let us also remember that we are Christians; that the Alleluias of Resurrection are ours; and that the wisest of Christian philosophers has bidden us: *Gaudete, Gaudete semper; iterum dico, gaudete!* And that a greater than St. Paul hath said: 'Can the children of the bridegroom mourn as long as the Bridegroom is with them?' And he is with us, so long as the eternal Sacrifice shall be offered – our Emmanuel, God with us, for ever!

The Apollyon of the Frost

We had a frost, a killing frost, last night. It came to beautify, and to destroy. It was a dread Apollyon under a virginal and beautiful disguise. A light snow sifted down from the gray sky in the late twilight; and the frost came and hardened it on the trees, until the leafless branches took on a perfect white plumage, and a great silence wrapped all the earth. The evergreens were more heavily coated than the trees whose foliage was deciduous, but these latter, where the snow fell thinner, and whose branches were thickly interlaced, looked very beautiful, although one felt that the loveliness was delicate and frail. One particular spot in my garden was a perfect marvel of beauty, so faint and fragile was the exquisite tracery on branches and tiny leaves. The sun came out, gave a new radiance to the landscape, and then dissolved the whole picture into weeping and wintry death again. And I marvelled at the magic of the frost, and all that it could do with that simple element of water, until my foot struck a dead thrush lying on the gravelled path. I took it up. It was frozen hard as a stone – all its spring music hushed for ever and destroyed. The same secret force that had created beauty, had annihilated it. I went into my greenhouse. All the plants that we had housed carefully for the Maytime, were wilted and withered. The magician of the frost and snow was the Apollyon of flower and bird.

The night cometh

What a singular coincidence it was that Johnson should have engraved on the dialplate of his watch, and Sir Walter Scott on the sun-dial in his garden the self-same words: νύξ γάρ ἔρχεται! For the night cometh! The former was constitutionally indolent; but this conscience was for ever protesting against it. The latter was seized with a passion for work, especially in the latter part of his life, within which he concentrated as much labour as was possible without straining the mind to the breaking-point. But this idea of work, as identical with life, seems to have seized on all great thinkers. It is their solution of the problem of the Universe – the one way of disen-tangling the threads of the mighty problem. *J'y suis!* And whatever my hands find to do, I shall do it with all my might. 'The night cometh!' So said the great Divine Teacher. Let me hasten then. It is no time for idle dreaming. Swiftly the little circle rounds to its close. To-day is mine; tomorrow is doubtful. Very soon I shall no longer be above the earth, but beneath it. Here, then, hand, eye, brain, lend your help! I need to leave behind me some record of my being. *Non omnis moriar!* There is a double sense in the words. I shall pass to a new existence, but shall remain on earth immortalized by my work. Its beneficent influences shall pass down the long valleys of the years, make sweet the bitter and fertile the barren, until men whose faces I shall never see shall bless the dead hand that grasped theirs from the grave! So think these great masters of thought. It is a noble ambition!

Work and worship

Yes, work and worship. There be the watchwords of that night which we call day. They are certainties, not merely possibilities – the certainties of that great monitor and task-master, Duty. Speculations are only useful in-asmuch as they lead on to work worship. Mere con-

jectures about the mystery of being would be fruitless
and profitless, if they ended with themselves in a cease-
less, unending round of difficulties propounded, only
to be postponed. But highest speculations resolve themselves, sooner or later, into the conclusion that, out of all
uncertainties and possibilities, one thing alone remains
positive and well-defined, and that is that our primal
obligations whilst we remain on this planet are worship
of the Invisible and Uncreated, and work of some kind
in the elements that go to make up life. For we, too,
have a kind of creative or conserving force within us.
And we have to evolve order and beauty out of sur-
roundings – the brown earth, the barren sea, the souls of
men; or we have to help in keeping intact such work as
the progressive centuries have wrought for mankind, and
to keep earth, and sea, and human lives from reverting
to primitive chaos.

Hesiod

That great line of Hesiod's:
      Ἔργα νεῶν, βουλαί τε μέσων, εὐχαί τε γερόντων,
is generally translated:

In the morning of life, work;
In the meridian of life, give counsel;
In the evening of life, pray.

Not bad for a pagan. Yet would it not be better to
say, pray in youth; work in middle life; give counsel
in old age? For, surely, youth needs prayer for enlightenment and strength, and distrust of self, and holy fear.
And it is in manhood, we work best, physically and
intellectually; for our energies do not reach their perfection till then, the wheels of life moving faster as we go
down the hill of time towards eternity. And it is the
tradition of mankind, that wisdom comes with age; for
if the cunning of Ulysses is lost, the experience of Nestor
supervenes; and grey-beard wisdom has a mellowness

that no ability, or study, or talent can give. The oil that flows down the beard of Aaron is holy, – holy with the balsam of experience, and consecrated by the years that have brought in their train the consecration of the Most High.

The Divine Teacher

When one has come to relish the sweetness and the strength of every word spoken by our Divine Lord to His disciples or the multitude, there is a holy impatience with the Evangelists for not having given the world more of that Divine wisdom. I have said when one has come to realize the sweetness and strength of the language of the Divine Teacher, because it needs experience and thought and comparison to understand how true was that expression of the wondering crowd: 'Never man spake like to this man!' I should say not. All human teaching in Dialogue, Enchiridia, Discourses, Pensées, Maxims, etc., sinks into ragged and beggarly insignificance before the wisdom of the Word. There can be nothing more foolish and banal, not to say irreverent, than to compare the teaching of any philosopher with the teaching of Christ. And hence there is no verse in all the Holy Scriptures so tantalizing to the followers of Christ as that last verse of the Gospel of St. John: 'But there are also many other things which Jesus did which, if they were written every one, the world itself, I think, would not be able to contain the books that should be written.' The Apostle might have added 'did and said,' for we know we have not a tithe of the sweet and beautiful discourses of our Lord. The recorded words are fragments, analecta, of long sermons in the Temple, by the sacred sea, on the mountains, by the wayside. Take the Sermon on the Mount. Do we not know that our Lord must have spoken long and earnestly before He summed up all in the deathless Beatitudes? And the discourse of the Last Supper – well, no! it would be hard to add anything to that! But it is certain that all that our Lord said in Nazareth and Judæa has not come down to us. Silence has fallen for ever on these sacred conferences, and no man can now reveal them!

Human teaching and Divine

Yet what would we not give for just a little more? What did He say when Lazarus went back to his sisters at Bethany, and all the wealth of love in that humble home was poured at His feet? What were the unspeakable confidences to His mother at Nazareth before He went out on His mighty mission? In what language did He pray to His Eternal Father from the solitude of the mountains and under the eternal stars? Would we not give up all the Socratic disputations for a tithe of these things that are now hidden from us? And Marcus Aurelius? And Seneca? Yes, and more! We would sacrifice Shakspere and Milton and Dante; and in these all merely human wisdom is enshrined – nay, we would make a holocaust of all the national literatures of the world, if the lips of the Evangelists could be unsealed, and if we could get ever so little of a deeper insight into the unspeakable and, alas! unrevealed depths of the soul of Christ!

George Eliot

George Eliot, in the first fervour of her apostasy from the Church, wrote thus to a friend:

I have many thoughts, especially on a subject I should like to work out: The superiority of the consolations of philosophy to those of (so-called) religion. Do you stare?

She did not carry out her pious design. She was young then, only thirty. Perhaps as the years went by, and experience took the spurs from enthusiasm, she thought better of it. Or perhaps wider reading than Strauss, or larger views than she found in the kiln-dried ethics of Spinoza, may have modified her views of philosophy as an active factor in life. Or perhaps, under trial, she may have found philosophy a broken reed. Like so many more, who in the intensity of human pride believe in Stoicism, she may have found it wanting. 'Sufficis tibi' sounds well; but music will not heal the wounds of the soul. 'Sufficit tibi gratia mea' sounds equally well, and it is the sovereign salve for broken or despairing humanity.

SECTION III.

Room for improvement

There is a large and ever-increasing class of people in these querulous and inquisitive times, who are forever demanding perfection everywhere except in themselves. One of these came into my garden yesterday. I take a little pride in my spring-flowers; and I expected to hear several notes of admiration. No. He was in the interrogatory mood. 'Why haven't you freesias? A garden is nothing without them. And the new American fuchsia is lovely. I hate these crocuses. They are vulgar things. How are your vines coming on? None! Do you mean to say you have no vines? Everyone now has vines. 'Tis a great mistake to pay four shillings a pound for grapes, when you can grow them yourself so easily.' 'Well,' I replied, 'I admit there is room for improvement. And a man should be grateful for such gratuitous advice as he gets from time to time. None of us is perfect. We are only aiming at perfection. In the near future, perhaps, when people will buy books, instead of borrowing them; and when this universal mendicancy into which our country has fallen (for if I am to judge by my daily post, we are in a state of hopeless insolvency and bankruptcy), has yielded to more hopeful or perhaps more honest conditions, I may be able to realize your ideals. And then I shall extend the field of my operations; and ask your permission to cultivate that half-acre of yours which now is growing a luxurious crop of dockweed and thistles.'

Crocuses

I would not mention in these philosophic pages such a trifling passage of arms, but for that remark about my crocuses. Now, I rather like these little crocuses. They come to you, just after the snowdrops, when all other

more gaudy things are hiding beneath the hard earth; and
they put up, and flaunt the little bit of colour which God
has given them, and just at the time when we want it
most sadly. I cannot help feeling grateful to them; but
after that remark of my friend's, I must confess, I began
to look askance at them. Vulgar? Well, I suppose they
are. And then came a curious association of ideas. That
word of contempt took me back in one flash of memory
to a scene I had once witnessed, more than a quarter of
a century before, in Dartmoor prison. I was in the prison
sacristy, vested for Mass. The bell had rung; and the
convicts were defiling past the sacristy door into their
places in the chapel. All had assembled; and my convict
acolyte had opened the door of the sacristy, when the
clank of chains smote upon me, and twelve or thirteen
prisoners, chained wrist to ankle, passed rapidly to the
door. They were clad in yellow, a bright but dirty yellow.
They were the dangerous prisoners, who had attempted
escape, or committed some fresh crime in prison.

Colour antipathies

There was something inexpressibly hideous about that
yellow convict garb. I had seen prisoners clad in parti-
colored yellow and brown, carefully mixed half and half.
It was only ludicrous. This complete yellow garb was
frightful. Then and there I conceived a violent aversion
to that colour. I discovered that it was also the emblem
of disease. The quarantine flag is yellow. I discovered
other abominations in connection with it. I wrote it down
as the outcast amongst colours, the symbol of all physical
and moral degeneracy. I found then that it was the Im-
perial colour in China. This only increased my aversion.
Then one day a friend (such a friend is never long wanting) reminded me that yellow was also the 'Turner'
colour; and futhermore, that it was the national colour of
the Irish, taken from their sunburst. Nay, that up to a
very recent period in their history, the Irish invariably
dyed their outer garment, a short, winged cloak, in

saffron! My discomfiture was complete. I tried to bluff him. I maintained that green was our national color; and, in pagan times, dark blue. He reminded me that within a stone's throw of this village is Saffron Hill, and that old men still remember the acres of yellow crocuses grown there to dye the cloaks of our ancestors.

The effect of Imagination

I began to believe then that yellow was unquestionably respectable, when that sudden, contemptuous remark sent me back to Dartmoor again; and the old sickening feeling of fear and repusion rose spectre-wise from the vault of memory. What creatures we are; and what slaves of our senses! I never knew a man who could picture to his imagination the whole of a ship at sea. In the dry dock it is easy enough. You see the entire hull, even to where it tapers away the bottom; you see the sharp edge, which, like the coulter of a plough, cuts the resisting waters; you see the great fin-like screw at the stern. But you see none of these things at sea. You see but the stately half-hull resting on the waves; and no more. And you cannot even imagine the rest. Try! And your fancy comes back at once to what your senses testify, and no more. So, in dealing with nature. We shudder with horror at the sensation of some harmless little thing creeping on our neck, or hand. We ruthlessly destroy it. We say it is hideous. Our sense of sight testifies that that beetle or earwig, is a monster of ugliness; and we instantly destroy it. What is all this? The knowledge of the senses? No! The ignorance, crass and stupid, of the senses. Look closer! Here, take this glass, and behold what a miracle of Omniscience you have trampled out of existence!

The magic of Poetry

'Now, now, now,' I hear some one say, 'this is absurd. Everyone knows you are credulous enough to believe a circus-poster; and sentimental enough to find poetry in an earth-worm.' I admit the soft impeachment. I do not believe that under the bell-tent of the circus you or I shall see all that appeared on the gaudy poster; but is it an exaggeration to the wondering eyes of childhood? Do not the children believe it all; and think the poster a wretched presentment of all the glories and Arabian Nights' splendours beneath the canvas? If I do not believe, so much the worse for me. I have become critical and analytical – the worse mental condition into which a human being can fall. But who will declare the poster to be exaggerated and untrue, when the children believe it all, even after their experience of the reality? It only proves the relativity of knowledge. But about the earth-worm! And poetry? How can you combine them? Well, genius can do everything. Did not Tennyson make poetry out of a veal-pasty in 'The Princess'? And if I disinter a now-forgotten poem from a forgotten poet, who once was so famous that this enthusiastic fellow-countrymen buried his masterpiece with him, I shall not be blamed; and there is one great picture where the despised earth-worm caps the climax of intensity.

Klopstock

I hear some witling say, 'buried his masterpiece with him.' A rather doubtful compliment, n'est-ce pas? No! It was a genuine compliment, such as his countrymen invariably pay to their immortals. The masterpiece was 'The Messiah,' the poet was Klopstock; the race was German. The lines ran thus:

... Earth grew still at the sinking twilight; the twilight
Gloomier; stiller the earth. Broad ghastly shadows, with pale
    gleams

Streaked more dimly and more, flowed troublous over the
   mountains.
Dumb withdrew the fowls of heaven to the depths of the
   forest;
Beasts of the field stole fearful to hide in the loneliest ca-
   verns.
Even the worm slunk down. In the air reigned deathlike
   silence.

I may be wrong, but I think that is a stroke of genius.
Our generation has gone into ecstasies over Tennyson's
minute observation of Nature and natural objects. The
colour of the ashbuds in the month of March, the slanting
way in which a lark sinks down on his nest, the lone
heron on the windy mere, the creeping of a wave along
the halls of a sea-cave – all have been noticed, and all
have been admired. But that line about the earth-worm
hiding itself in the convulsions of Nature under the horrors of the Crucifixion has haunted me from the day I
read it, many years ago, in Taylor's *Survey of German
Poetry.*

Goethe

Klopstock, I believe, has long since gone out of fashion
even in his native Germany. And Carlyle, for us, has long
since dethroned him; and enthroned his own godkin,
Goethe, in his place. I confess, I cannot whip my mind
into a ferment of enthusiasm about Goethe; just as I
cannot bend the knee to Burns, or other Philistine deity.
I have conscientiously tried and failed. I have read
through *Elective Affinities,* and *Wilhelm Meister's Ap-
prenticeship,* and the rest. It was weary work, lightened
only by the Ariel-presence and ever-to-be-remembered
song of Mignon. The world will ever be grateful to
Goethe for that. It is a breath of spring air amid mephitic
vapours – the carol of a bird, suddenly heard on an
artificial, gas-lighted, meretricious stage. Indeed,
Goethe's masterpieces are his lyrics. The Mason-song,

made familiar by Carlyle's translation; and the song of the Parcæ in *Iphigenia* are likely to endure. But I have a shrewd suspicion that the good court-ladies who crowned him with laurel-wreaths in his old age, and after the performance of that same drama, had in mind his wonderful masculine beauty, as well as the splendours of his genius. And I also think *Faust* has captivated the world not for its philosophy, which is jejune enough; nor for its morality, which is invisible; nor for its art, which is weak in the opening scenes of the First Part, and in every scene of the Second; but for its tender tale of human love and sorrow.

Schiller

For just the opposite reason, Schiller never reached the popularity of his friend and rival. What deceptive things portraits, especially photographs, are! For more than a quarter of a century, I have had a photograph of Schiller in my album; and I had formed the idea of a poetic face and form, more than Byronic in its beauty. The firm set of the features, clear-cut and Grecian in their outline, the long hair streaming in ringlets on the shoulders, the bold, flashing eye, and the proud curved lip, gave on the idea of a self-reliant world-despising intellectual giant. Alas! life is all a disillusion! I read in later life the following, and was most reluctantly undeceived:

In his bedroom we saw his skull for the first time, and were amazed at the smallness of the intellectual region. There is an intensely interesting sketch of Schiller lying dead, which I saw for the first time in the study; but all pleasure in thinking of Schiller's portraits and bust is now destroyed to me by the conviction of their untruthfulness. Rauch told us he had a *miserable Stirne*. Waagen says that Tieck, the sculptor, told him there was something in Schiller's whole person that reminded him of a *camel*.*

* *Life of George Eliot.*

74

No enthusiasm, certainly no feminine enthusiasm, would be proof against this! And when you add to this, that he had a *Gänsehals* (gooseneck), the disillusion is complete.

Great writers and the Church

It is strange how great minds invariably turn, by some instinct or attraction, towards this eternal miracle – the Church. Carlyle admits in his extreme old age that the Mass is the most genuine act of religious belief left in the world. Goethe was for ever introducing the Church into his conversations, coupling it with the idea of power, massive strength, and ubiquitous influence. Byron would insist that his daughter, Allegra, should be educated in a convent, and brought up a Catholic, and nothing else. And Ruskin, although he did say some bitter things about us, tells us what a strong leaning he has towards monks and monasteries; how he pensively shivered with Augustinians at St. Bernard; happily made hay with Franciscans at Fiesole; sat silent with the Carthusians in their little gardens south of Florence; and mourned through many a day-dream at Bolton and Melrose. Then he closes his little litany of sympathy with the quaintly Protestant conclusion: But the wonder is always to me, not how much, but how little, the monks have on the whole done, with all that leisure, and all that goodwill.

Ruskin

He cannot understand! That is all. But why? Because he cannot search the archives of Heaven. He knows nothing of the supernatural – of the invisible work of prayer – of work that is worship. He has never seen the ten thousand thousand words of praise that have ascended to the Most High; and the soft dews of graces innumerable that have come down from Heaven in answer to prayer. He has painted, as no one else, except perhaps Carlyle could, the abominations of modern life; and he has flung all the strength of his righteous anger against them. He has never asked himself why God is so patient, whilst John Ruskin rages; or why fire and brimstone are not showered from Heaven, as whilom on the Cities of the Plain. He had read his Bible, year by year, hard words, Levitical laws, comminatory Psalms, from ἔν αρχῆ to Amen; and, what is more rare, he believed in it. Yet he never tried to fathom the mystery of the unequal dealings of God with mankind. He never saw the anger of the Most High soothed, and His hand stayed by the midnight prayer and scourge of the Trappist and the Carthusian. Dante could never have written the *Paradiso*, if he had not heard Cistercians chanting at midnight!

Work and Prayer

So, too, he failed to understand how a mountain-monk would positively refuse to go into raptures about crags and peaks and fix his thoughts on eternity. 'I didn't come here to look at mountains,' was the abrupt answer of the stern monk to the nineteenth-century æsthete. What then? You must think of something my shaven friend, or go mad. 'I thought of the ancient days; I had in mind the eternal fears,' was the reply. Very profitless employment, certainly, to the eyes of modern wisdom, which believes that 'work is worship;' but that worship is not work. How can it be, when you see no visible results – no piling up of shekels, nor hoisting of sky-scrapers, no hoggish slaughter-houses, nor swinish troughs; only psalms that die out in the midnight darkness, and silent prayer from lonely cell away on that snow-clad mountain summit.

The Contemplative Orders

I notice that this is the one feature in Catholicity which the Protestant mind can never understand. It appreciates cordially the Catholic work of rescue – the rescue of the waif from the street, of the Magdalen from the gaol or river, of the drunkard from the bottle, of the gambler from the table, of the orphan from destitution and vice. And so it will tolerate, but only tolerate, educational or charitable institutions or communities – what we call the Active Orders. But the Contemplative Orders it cannot understand. Why a number of monks and nuns should be shut up in cloistered seclusion, cut away from all sympathy with human life and endeavour, apparently unproductive and useless factors in the great giant march of progress, in unintelligible. Of course, it is! Because God is unintelligible, or rather ignored. Because all modern religion, outside into humanitarianism – that is positivism – that is, atheism in its crudest and most naked aspect.

God, or man?

In fact, all controversy between the Church and the world is rapidly resolving itself into this: Is God to be placed in the foreground of His universe; or is man? The Church strenuously affirms the former; the world the latter. The Church says, God is everything; man, nothing, except in God. God, the centre to which all things tend, and from which all things radiate; man not the apex of creation by any means, only a unit in creation, made sublime by his aspirations, his hopes, his sufferings, and his destiny. A generation that has lost all faith in Thirty-nine Articles or other formulary, seeks vainly for something that will take the place of vanished beliefs. The next thing to hand is humanity – man, the little god of this planet. *Agnoscimus!* we know no more! And the eternal Church keeps tolling its bell through the world; and the burden of its persistent calling is the monotone of Time, echoed from Eternity: God, and God, and God!

George Eliot and Protestantism

George Eliot, too, that fine mind, darkened, alas! so early to all that was really sublime, had a curious sympathy with Catholic faith and worship. She bitterly laments the fact that Nürnberg has become Protestant; and that it had but one Catholic Church, where one could go in and out as one would. She goes into the Protestant St. Sebald's, where a clergyman was reading in a cold formal way under the grand Gothic arches. Then she enters the Catholic Frauen-Kirche, where the organ and voices were pealing forth a glorious Mass. 'How I loved the good people around me, as we stood with a feeling of brotherhood amongst the standing congregation till the last notes of the organ had died out.' And at her first glance at the Sistine Madonna, as she sat on the sofa, opposite that miracle of art, a 'sort of awe, as if I were suddenly in the living presence of some glorious being, made my heart swell too much for me to remain comfortably and we hurried out of the room.' Probably, the finest testimony ever given by a subtle and refined temperament to the magic of art! One could forgive a good deal to that spontaneous act of veneration.

Her teaching

By the way, what a singular chapter in the history of literature is her life and works and destiny. Even during her lifetime she had as many commentators as Shakspere. Her peculiarly masculine intellect, which took up and discussed with ease, begotten of conscious mastery of the subject, problems in human life which might have puzzled Plato, had apparently fascinated modern thought, and made her the idol of a generation which prides itself upon being, above all things, intellectual. It would be a marvel, indeed, if in all the hero-worship of which she was the object, there were not a fair amount of extravagance. It is easy enough to exaggerate the merits of a writer who has excited our wonder by powers of observation – shall we say creation? – that were unique. And there was a very strong temptation to see even beyond the vision of the writer, and to conjecture deep suggestion and lofty wisdom beneath apparently simple elements. Goethe's *Faust* is supposed to be a revelation of mysteries hitherto unguessed, and which the initiated only can read. I have heard it styled 'The Bible of Freemasonry.' Tennyson's Idylls are supposed to be essentially allegorical, the meaning of the allegory being sealed, notwithstanding his own revelations, until some generation shall arise more mature in its wisdom than ours. And George Eliot is supposed to have given us not only a system of philosophy, but even a religion, in her writings, the key of which lies with the future; and then – the millennium!

Above the de Staëls and Sévignés

The truth appears to be that she was a woman of singular natural gifts, and with a taste for subjects and studies which belong traditionally to the masculine mind. In fact, she stands alone among her sex for her brilliant enterprises in the highest sphere of philosophic thought, her marvellous knowledge of the human heart and its workings, and a power of analyzing human thoughts and feelings, which is unique in modern literature. In the golden age of French literature many brilliant women thronged the *salons* of Paris – great wits, great conversationalists, and amateurs in the sceptical philosophy which was just then becoming fashionable. But none of them essayed to be what George Eliot has become. She towers above the de Staëls and Sévignés as Shakspere above a troubadour.

Her types

Altogether she is, perhaps, the most remarkable figure in modern literature. Her life was very tranquil, yet she paints very passionate scenes. She passed through few of the vicissitudes which make life tragic for the sufferer, yet she realizes them as clearly as Jane Welsh Carlyle. The world has long been wondering how Charlotte Brönté, a simple country girl, brought up in the seclusion of a Yorkshire parsonage, could have even conceived such a character as Rochester. But much more surprising is the fact that Marian Evans, reared in the quiet monotony of a country life, could, by sheer powers of fancy, and without having seen a single type of her creations among men and women (if we except her clerical characters), evolve such opposite characters as Silas Marner and Tito, or such types of religious enthusiasm as Savonarola and Dinah Morris.

A kind of Pallas Minerva

And she writes without apparently one bit of sympathy with her creations. There is a tone through all her works as of one who looks upon the eccentricities of humanity with the pitying contempt of a being far removed above them. It is as if Pallas had come down to earth, and framed out of her wisdom these strange puppets of humanity, and paraded them before us, and said: 'Behold! these be types of women and men; mark how they speak and act! I will tell you every motion that stirs them, every passion that excites them; I will lay bare their minds and hearts, and perhaps you will see some things which you yourself have experienced.'

Her latent Religion

It is absolutely certain, however, that this rare genius did retain to the end of life all her religious instincts and sympathy, although, alas! she broke away from all religious beliefs. She loathed her task of translating the *Leben Jesu* of Strauss, and loathed still more the asperity and bitterness of the author. Could anything be more significant and pathetic than her confession that she could only find strength and resolution to write the story of Crucifixion by gazing on a figure of the Crucified that surmounted her desk? Could anything be more admonitory than her old-age admission that the basis of all happiness consists in possessing definite religious beliefs? Could anything be more reassuring than her attachment to the Bible (although Lewes repudiated it with scorn) to the end, and the fact that the *Imitation of Christ* lay upon her bed when she was dying; and that these two books, the inspired and the semi-inspired, with that *Commedia* that all men have agreed to call Divine, were the constant companions of her senility and illness? Could anything be more terrible to the votaries of humanitarianism than her confession to her friend as they passed up and down Addison's Walk at Oxford: 'I see no hope for humanity but one grand, simultaneous act of suicide'?

Nemesis

It is strange, too, how the old Greek idea of Fate, under the form of a Nemesis, or Retribution, not to be propitiated or averted, became a leading dogma of her life. It is the leading idea in Spinoza's Ethics; Strauss accepted it; Emerson formulated it thus: –

The specific stripes may follow late upon the offence; but they follow, because they accompany it. Crime and punishment grow out of one stem. We cannot do wrong, without suffering wrong.

81

This doctrine might be controverted. It might be accepted as a kind of halting Christianity; it might even do good to be so accepted and preached, always with the scholium – that crime is not unpardonable with God, if it is unforgivable by Nature and Society. But the curious thing is, that the most violent opponents of dogma are obliged to fall back upon dogma in the end; and the Naturalism would find it difficult to explain the secret power that makes for Retribution, whilst it denies the Higher Intelligence that can punish or pardon according to Its own supreme decrees.

Resignation and Activity

Probably, this was the reason why George Eliot adopted as a practical maxim of life that Comtist doctrine: *Notre vraie destinée se compose de resignation et d'activité.* Work, work, work. Work blindly, but unceasingly. You will blunder; nay, you will criminate yourself. And behind you is Nemesis with her whip of scorpions. You cannot escape the lash. You are the galley-slave, with the cannon-ball tied to your ankle, and the warder over you with whip or musket, and the oar in your bleeding hands. What then? Well, then, you must be resigned. There is no mending matters. It is Fate. There is one hope – the grave. Tears and prayers and penance are unavailing. The Fates are inexorable. They cannot be moved aside. There is no repentance; only Retribution. So says Nature in every tone. And we are Nature's children. We cannot say *Our Father*, for we have none. Let us take up our work, then, and go silently forward. And if the lash falls, let us yield to it, and swallow our tears with our bread. This is life, and there is none other.

The Nemesis of Sin

Did she suffer, I wonder, from the retribution she preached? She violated the universal law in her pretended marriage with George Henry Lewes. What was the penalty? A certain biographer puts it – 'the estrangement of friends, the loss of liberty of speech, the foremost rank amongst the women of her country, and a tomb in Westminster Abbey.' Did she feel all this? Or was the pleasure of perfect domestic felicity and a happy fireside a compensation? We cannot think so. A note of depression runs through all the records of her married life. She seems to be always deprecating criticism; always watching the faces of her visitors. How poor a thing is philosophy, or logic, in face of a violated law! How disgusting the very apologies that men make for the emancipation of passion from law! Her great author, Feuerbach, asserted that enjoyment is a duty; and that it was the merest affectation to turn away from immodest or indecent scenes. Strauss sneered at the text which laid down the law of Christian chastity. Rousseau praised Sophie for her sin. Are not these grave and reverend personages, whose authority is all-sufficing? Alas, no! Society is inexorable; Nature is arbitrary, and Conscience imperative. There is no escaping the Nemesis of Sin, except by Repentance.

The Mystery of Pain

The existence of evil in the world is a stumbling-block to many philosophers who cannot understand how inevitable in their own theories it is in a world of limitations and finite beings. The existence of pain is a still greater mystery to those who refuse to believe that it has its own wonderful secrets, which might well be purchased at even a dearer price. Pain, that purifies the victim, preaches to the strong, and evolves in victims and helpers virtues of which they were not even cognizant. For if it be true what a certain French cynic has said, that there is something in our worst misfortunes which does not altogether displease our nearest friends, let this be understood not in the sense that they rejoice in our misery, but in the sense of relief that they themselves have been spared so much pain. But for those who are closer and dearer, that seemingly selfish satisfaction does not obtain. Nay, they would gladly change places with us on our beds of pain, from which we preach to them the charity which they practise to us, and give even to the selfish the pleasure of immunity from the evils that afflict ourselves.

Epicurean and Intellectual

George Eliot did not escape the common lot. She suffered; but her suffering made her neither strong, nor interesting. It was the suffering of a well-to-do dyspeptic. One cannot sympathize well with this lady, whose drawing room was turned into a cave of the Sybil, where she sat at the left-hand side of the fireplace, and awed visitors trod lightly on the soft carpet, as they were ushered into her presence, with a kind of admonitory reverence by her second husband and biographer. And if they thought at the same time of the enormous cheques that lay in her bureau from her publishers – £10,000 for one novel £5,000 for another, and so on – somehow it must have mitigated their apprehensions, diluted her philosophy, and dulled their heroine-worship. And yet, perhaps, this is wrong. Nothing succeeds like success; and there is no success, to some minds, if the final chaplet does not fall from the hands of Mammon. But this easy though busy life, unbroken by alternations of struggle and stress, is not what one expects from literary giants; it is too epicurean and intellectual to be interesting. One misses the plaint.

Ah! who can tell how hard it is to climb
The steep where Fame's proud temple shines afar?

The struggles of Genius

I confess I am more interested in that painful, uphill struggle, which most literary men have to face, and of which Richter most probably speaks (for it was his own experience) when he says:

But often wilt thou shed thine own blood, that thou mayst the more firmly step down the path that leads to old age, even als chamois-hunters support themselves by the blood of their own heels.

This suffering and struggle give strength and enlightenment. You cannot really understand life until you have tasted the sense of *camaraderie* that comes from drinking out of the same bottle and sharing the same crust, – I was near saying, and occupying in the same branch, like that Bohemian who gave his town address as

Avenue de St. Cloud, third tree to the left after leaving the Bois de Boulogne, and fifth branch.

Isn't that delightful? And imagine those starving geniuses, – Balzac, Chenier, Murger, Karol, or some such like, bending over the ashes of their manuscripts which they had ignited to keep up a little heat, when the snow lay thick on Nôtre-Dame, and the mercury was some hundreds of degrees below zero!

The thorns of Literature

All successful writers are unanimous in warning off young aspirants from the thorny path of literature. Grant Allen would give them a broom, and bid them take to crossing-sweeping; Gibbon, de Quincey, Scott, Southey, Lamb, Thackeray, – all showed the weals and lashes of the hard taskmaster; amongst moderns, Daudet warns that brain-work is the most exacting of all species of labour, and must eventuate, sooner or later, in a bad break-down; Mr. Zangwill says, somewhat grandiosely: 'Whoso with blood and tears would dig art out of his soul, may lavish his golden prime in pursuit of emptiness; or striking treasure, find only fairy gold, so that when his eye is purged of the spell of morning, he sees his hand is full of withered leaves.' And dear old Sam Johnson, who certainly passed through his Inferno and Purgatorio before he settled down in the confortable paradise at Streatham, epitomizes his hardships as author in the well-known line.

Toil, envy, want, the patron, and the gaol.

Ambition

Nor can all these aspirants claim the steady nerve and calm philosophy of Jean Paul, who can see in poverty but 'the pain of piercing a maiden's ears, that you may hang precious jewels in the wound.' It is a bitter thing, a serve initiation into mysteries otherwise unintelligible; and hence it is, I suppose, that with the eternal hope of youth, the ambitious see but the goal and the prize; and like Alpine climbers, undismayed by the fate of others, and utterly oblivious of danger, they refuse to see crevasse or avalanche, or sliding glacier. They only see the peaks far away, shining like amber in the morning sun; and they promise themselves that at evening, they shall stand on that summit where no foot of mortal had ever trodden before. It is somewhat melancholy; and yet it is the one thing that gives to the biographical part of literature that interest, amounting to sympathy, which is the right of the strong, who have fought their way through difficulties to success.

Balzac and his sister

It would be well, however, that this sympathy took a practical turn, especially where genius is concerned; and I know no more touching instance of this inspiring hopefulness than the letters of his sister Laura to Balzac. She stood by him and encouraged him, when his parents turned him from the door as a fool, because he gave up the comfortable profession of notary, and took to the dry crusts and rags of literature; she sympathized with all his struggles, rejoiced in all his triumphs; she advised him, controlled him, encouraged him; and she stood by his bedside on that fatal day, August 18, 1850, when, after thirty hours of fearful agony, he died in the city that refused to recognise his talents till after death. A lurid, tempestuous, passionate life – misdirected and misapplied! His biographer told the truth when he said that Paris was a hell, but a hell, the only place worth living in; and of this he vowed to be a Dante. He succeeded but too well; and it would have been better for him and the world if he had left the secrets unrevealed. But, at least, Laura was his Beatrice.

Bohemians

Poor Henry Murger, too! All that one can remember of him is his mother's intense devotion; his horrible disease, *purpura*, which he laughingly declared he wore with the dignity of a Roman Emperor; his chivalric devotion to the Sister of Charity who nursed him in hospital – 'A good Sister you were, the Beatrice of that hell. Your soothing consolations were so sweet, that we all complained whenever we had the chance, so as only to be consoled by you;" – his anticipation of O. W. Holmes' poem, 'The Voiceless':

Nous avons cru pouvoir – nous l'avons cru souvent
Formuler notre rêve, et le rendre vivant
    Par la palette ou par la lyre;

Mais le souffle manquait, et personne n'a pu
Deviner quel était le poëme inconnu
    Que nous ne savions pas traduire.

Then, his childish warning off the priests. 'Tell them I have read Voltaire.' Finally his cry: 'Take me to the Church; God can do more than any physician.' His final happy death, after receiving the last Sacraments. Poor fellows! with their sad motto: The Academy, the Asylum, or the Morgue! How the hearts of a Vincent de Paul, or a Philip Neri, would have yearned over your helplessness and your genius, and wept for your follies and your sins! And how lesser folk would have liked to burst into your attic, and tear your valuable papers from the fire, and send ruddy blazes out of more ready material dancing up the chimney; and pelted you with sandwiches till you cried, Hold! and then sat down with you on a soap box or on your dingy bed; and filled out in long ruby glasses the Margaux or Lafitte you had not tasted for many a day; and finally settled down to a calm, long, soporific smoke, and listened to the song, the anecdote, the *bon mot,* that would turn the gloom of Phlegethon into an Attic night, and the lentils of a Daniel into a supper of the gods!

Pascal

Pascal, too, found a rare helper and sympathizer in his sister, – the Madame Perrier, who wrote his life so briefly, but significantly. Not, indeed, that he needed any spiritual strength or support from any external power; for he was a self-contained spirit, and thought little of human help. And his genius was colossal. Like Aristotle he seems to have thought out a whole scheme of creation, unaided. It is rather a singular instance of human folly that he should have been considered a sceptic. There is no stopping the tongues of men. The same charge was levelled against Dr. Newman. Mozeley attributes the great popularity of the Oratorian in England to that.

Perhaps there were never two men who believed more intensely and unreservedly. But the Frenchman lacked serenity. He lost his nobility by engaging, not so much in a lost cause, as a bad cause. He descended to cynicism and sarcasm – the expression of a form of lower mental condition. And this, too, affected his greatest, if most imperfect work. When the *Provincial Letters* are forgotten or neglected as splenetic sarcasm, and have passed away like the Junius and Drapier Letters, and have become but the study of the connoisseur, his 'Pensées' will remain, broken fragments of an incomplete, but immortal work.

The judgment of posterity

What judgment will posterity pass on them? It would be difficult to say. But if we may gauge the future by the present, we would say that the verdict of a more enlightened age than ours will be, that Pascal was no sceptic, though a bold inquirer; that his marvellous mental keenness and vigour were only equalled by his rigid asceticism; that Nature had made him pious, and circumstances made him proud; that these 'Thoughts' which reveal to us his inner life are beautiful and deep beyond words; that they would have even the colour of that inspiration which comes from Nature and Grace united, were it not for a dark shadow which stretches itself over all, making the philosophy of them less clear, the truth of them less apparent, the study of them a task of anxiety and suspicion, instead of being one of edification and delight.

Renan and his sister

In fact, I know but of one case where a sister's influence was hurtful; and that was the case of Ernest Renan. It is impossible to explain how a woman, and a Bretonne, could have lent the aid of her sisterly influence to wean

89

him away from the sanctuary, and then from the Church itself. There is something inexpressibly revolting about it, because I think, of all human loves, that of a sister is the most abiding and unselfish. In a mother's love there is a kind of identification with her child, his triumphs, his defeats, which, by the reflection on herself, takes away the absolute disinterestedness. Conjugal love is more intense, but for that reason more intermittent. But there's not a trace of self in that earnest wistful gaze which a beloved sister casts after the poor young fellow who has just gone out from the sanctity of home-life into the world's arena; nor a thought of self in the way the silent heart broods over shattered hopes, and takes back to its sanctuary the broken relics of the idol, once worshipped, now, alas! only to be protected from the gaze of a scornful world.

Lengthening days

Post tenebras lux! The motto, of all places on earth, of the city of Geneva! Well, no matter. Here is light now in early spring, or rather in expiring winter; and it is very welcome. For much as I love my fire and lamp, there is a certain regeneration in body and soul and spirits, in these days which are lengthening out, bit by bit, as the sun ascends higher in the heavens, and the dawn breaks earlier, and the twilight lingers even in the steel-blue sky. Winter is still here. The sirocco-breath of the east wind withers all vegetation, and seems to dry the very blood in the veins of men. Delicate people crouch all day by their fires; and look out despairingly at the gray, mournful skies, and the earth parched and hardened by the wind. And yet there is hope; and the days are drawing out, and the nights are shortening; and there is light, light; and we feel we are rushing on to the time when the summer twilight will fade away only to break out into the resurrection of a roseate summer dawn.

The equilibrium of the Universe

I could not help feeling this evening, as the great red shield of the moon rose solemnly above the trees, and Jupiter hung like a dewdrop in a purled sky, that it should be a great consolation for us to know, that whatever may befall us, little creatures of God, – death, life, sorrow, joy, – the great wheel of existence swings in its beautiful and perfect equilibrium before the face of God; and that even when we shall have departed hence, and our place shall know us no more, there never shall be rift nor break in that cosmical perfection of sun, and star, and season, that seems to know its own beauty, and to exult in it before the face of its Maker. 'When the morning stars sang together,' may be more than a figure of speech; and it is something to know that, above this little globe of sorrow, which we so strangely call 'the valley of tears,' the great universe is swinging softly and majestically; and that neither Time, nor Death, the two great solvents, can wither the beauty, or tarnish the lustre of all those other creatures of Omnipotence that are so far beyond the reach of our powers to comprehend; but not beyond the scope of reason to imagine, or interpret.

The tendency to perfection

Then I began to consider, why did that thought strike me just then, and not at any other time? I had seen burning noons and glorious sunsets without number; I had watched the faint sickle of the new moon in the West, and thanked her for her benevolence, when, gibbous and hunchbacked and unbeautiful, she made all things beneath her beautiful. But this idea of the symmetry and perfection and harmony of Creation had not struck me so forcibly before. Then I remembered that it was but imperfect moons and declining suns I had seen. The former excluded all idea of rounded and perfected beauty; the latter, with all their splendours, were the funereal accompaniments of the death of day. But this

91

great, red moon, burning through the latticed trees, and then paling away as it mounted higher and higher in heaven, was a symbol of the perfect beauty to which all things tend; and it rose in the night-dawn, young and beautiful, and with all the promise of uninterrupted empire all through the silent but eloquent watches of the night, until the white dawn came, and it would fade away, silent as a ghost, down the long avenues of paling stars, towards its grave in the West.

Optimism

You see then, to be an optimist you must have two associations – youth and the idea of ultimate perfection. Hence every child is an optimist, believing that all things are fair and beautiful; and absolutely idealizing the ugliest things until they put on the wings and outlines of perfect and immaculate loveliness. It is the glorious exaggeration of imagination without experience to clip its wings and bring it down to earth. It is only when the wheels of life begin to move more slowly, as they get clogged and debilitated, that we begin to take analytical views of life; and as our shadows lengthen in the sunset, we allow the past to project its gloom athwart our life-path, until it ends in the near perspective of the tomb. Then, we begin to reason, and shake our heads mournfully, and speculate, and haply become merely resigned. But the full tide of life creeps slowly through our veins; and we begin to pity our far-off selves, who in the imprudence and inexperience of youth, we remember to have been intoxicated with the delirium of life, and to have said aloud, or to our own hearts: All is fair and beautiful; and all is well!

Then, too, we must have the idea, so uncommon, so slippery, so often confuted, and as often revived, that all things round to final perfection. It needs a healthy brain, or well-defined religious principles, to comprehend it. The whole of literature seems to be a wail of protest it. Now and again, a great optimist, bravely cheers us onward with an expression of faith, like the song of Pippa; or the lines:

There shall never be one lost good! What was shall live as
    before;
  The evil is null – is naught – is silence implying sound;
What was good, shall be good, with, for evil, so much good
    more;
  On the earth, the broken arcs; in the heaven, a perfect
    round.

But this is rare! Even when Tennyson seeks to lift his verse on the wings of hope, he finds they are broken, and he falls to earth and sorrow again. And yet, there is no word so detested by men as that word 'pessimism'; nor is there any verdict so dreaded by those teachers colled philosophers and poets, as the sentence that their teaching is pessimistic. How is this? With so strong a tendency towards the evil thing, how is it that men so much dread the evil reputation? Yet, when you come to consider it, you will find that these writers, one and all, fall into that dreadful category of St. Paul: 'Without God, and with no hope in this world.'

Ensemblists

On the other hand, you will find that the teachers who point with hope to this final perfection, even though they do not belong to the household of the faith, seem to be carried, almost in spite of themselves, along the current of pure, intellectual thought, towards it. All the terrible contradictions of life seem to merge into one great unification; and that is, that the great positives of life, – virtue, holiness, happiness, health, – are the realities that abide, and continue with a perpetual and seemingly unconscious bias, or rather destiny, towards final perfection; and that the negatives, – sin, vice, disease, death, – although obstructions, can never pass beyond their negative form; and finally fade away, or are merged in their positives, until Evil disappears; and there only remain the Beautiful and the Good. These thinkers, whom some call *Ensemblists,* or those who view Life and the Universe as a whole, come very close to the poet who sings:

> for somehow good
> Shall be the final goal of ill;

and very near the Apostle of the *Gaudetes,* who assures 'that the sorrows of this life are not to be compared with the glory to come that shall be revealed in us.'

Failure of Hegelianism

But this dream of final perfection and loveliness, after all, is it a forecast of what shall be in the final evolution of our species; or rather is it not the noble and cherished tradition of a race that once possessed it, and lost it? It would be difficult for the Hegelian school to construct a scheme where all things would round to perfection, considering that they place their theories on the finite and limited nature of things, which therefore are necessarily imperfect; and from whose very essence arise the concomitants of imperfection – sin, disease, death. Hegel denies the immortality of the soul, except in the restricted and unsatisfactory sense of an absorption in the Universal of the individual. But how we are to pass the bounds of imperfection, that is limitation, and reach to the Unlimited, the Perfect, he cannot say. And with the more modern evolutionist theory, the idea is still more intangible and difficult to seize. The slow processes of the suns have not brought us far on the road to final perfection. There is evil – disease, vice, death. Has the horizon of human hope a gleam of a better land beyond it; or do not rather the shadows darken as we approach, without the lamp of faith, that bourn of all human sufferings and joys, where the shadows of death encompass us, and the perils of hell may find us?

Humanity fallen to rise again

On the other hand, how noble is the tradition, that we did possess that perfection to which all things tend, but fell from it; that therefore, final perfection is not the lurid dream of insensate beasts, so much as the far foreshadowing of what must be, because it once was; that, therefore, being fallen, we have the power of rising again to the heights whence we were precipitated; and, above all, we are not a race, moving on to the goal, and sifting itself of all its weaker elements, so that in the survival of the fittest, its dreams of ambition may be attained. But the majesty of the individual soul shines out conspicuous in the lofty scheme of rehabilitation and resurrection; and race-abstractions, race-destinations, &c., give place to the supreme importance that attaches to each single creation of the Almighty in His scheme of universal redemption. When we speak, therefore, of the tendency of all things to final perfection, we mean the recovery of lost rights and happiness, lost dignities and glory; and these not incommensurate with our state; but our righteous privileges and prerogatives, which the sin of our ancestors forfeited; but which we may, through the sacrifice of our Elder Brother, gloriously win back again.

First published in the Netherlands.
Made and printed in Holland by Van Boekhoven-Bosch nv, Utrecht